KILLING JUSTICE

A LAWYER LANDS IN PRISON AND FINDS HIS FREEDOM

KELLY GILES

ADVANCE PRAISE FOR KILLING JUSTICE

"Kelly Giles descends from the highs of being an attorney to the lows of being a felon. He creates Kel-Dar, his version of Vonnegut's Billy Pilgrim, in an attempt to escape the absurdity of his life. He's also trying to escape his feelings of never belonging, from having been adopted from a foster home at eleven months by Mom and Pops. But his long overdue diagnosis of PTSD finally helps him understand that belonging is overrated, and that his seven year old darkly comic sci-fi storyteller self is in need of resurrection."
   —Andy Behrman, author of *Electroboy: A Memoir of Mania*

"The prison pages reminded me of Hunter S. Thompson."
   —Judit Maull, film & TV Producer, Happy Madison Productions

"Killing Justice is a rollercoaster that will have you hoping this is just fiction during the most painful moments, but it will also have you grateful that it is a true story when you see the rainbow after the storm. I highly recommend this memoir for inspiration, knowledge, and hope. It is a real, godly, and magnificent read. Imperfectly perfect."
   —Deanna Pak, actress, filmmaker, and author of *Hungry in Hollywood: How to Be a Working Actor*

"Justice is considered to be one of the hallmarks of freedom in a democracy, but the convoluted system that we live under often fails, taking away a freedom that most of us take for granted. Killing Justice chronicles the heartfelt story of Kelly Giles, an honest man victimized by this tragic failure of the justice system, who managed to overcome the adversity of wrongful incarceration, and ultimately found his way to true freedom."
   —Matthew J. Pallamary, author of *Land Without Evil and Spirit Matters*

"This book is a roller coaster ride of someone who was working for justice and safety for those who were oppressed and then became a victim of injustice himself while doing so. It is inspiring to know there are lawyers like Kelly Giles who did not seek wealth or power but rather dedicated himself to work to rescue those who are poor and powerless…One of the great mysteries of life is often around the question of why do bad things happen to good people—and Kelly's journey is one of those mysteries—but ends with some answers to the mystery and his moving forward despite the hurdles thrown at him by life's challenges."

—Bill Watanabe, community organizer and former director of Little Tokyo Service Center

"Kelly provides us with the details required to be immersed in this harrowing story of how an attorney's life exploded into a nightmare. We walk with him as he begins to understand how he became linked, unknowingly, to a criminal enterprise that led to incarceration. We support him as he analyzes how his lifelong desperation to belong, which had driven him to become a lawyer, eventually led to the end of that career. And we root for him as he finds a new path forward."

—Judge Mary Beth O'Connor, author of *From Junkie to Judge: One Woman's Triumph Over Trauma and Addiction*

*"*Killing Justice *is at turns tragic, haunting, and ultimately, inspirational. Giles takes the reader on a powerful journey which shows how truth, faith, and love can overcome damn near anything.*

Kelly Giles is a lawyer, but not the kind you see on television or film: he works behind the scenes, keeps his head down, and is totally focused on providing top-notch legal representation for his clients– immigrants hoping for a new life in the United States. But that noble role falls apart one day when Giles is greeted by men with guns, waiting to arrest him at the airport. Killing Justice *explains not only how this cliffhanger beginning came to be, but also what came after, and how Giles was able to rebuild his life in the aftermath of a horrible betrayal. The structure of this memoir, in particular, makes for page-turning momentum—Giles splits the narrative between multiple time periods, parceling out enough information and backstory to keep you riveted, but in short enough bursts to keep the pace rolling. I found* Killing Justice *to be a standout memoir, as well, because Giles*

doesn't examine the past through rose-colored glasses; there are dark lessons that are not shied away from or glossed over, and he freely admits many times there were things he could have (and should have) done differently. And like after the best examples of the form, by the end of Giles' memoir, I was re-thinking my own views on the criminal justice system, faith, and what it takes to endure a personal hell. Killing Justice *is an engaging, revealing look at a life totally upended by fraud and injustice—and how that life was reclaimed."*
  —Trey Dowell, author of *The Protectors*

"In Killing Justice, *Kelly Giles explores the idealism of an immigration attorney caught in a web of mock justice and the soul crushing search into his own psyche to rekindle his shattered faith in himself and humanity."*
  —D.M. Peterson, M.A., author and educator

"Kelly Giles' Killing Justice: A Lawyer Lands in Prison and Finds his Freedom *is a gripping tale that grabs hold of you from the very start and refuses to let go. It's a poignant exploration of life's unexpected twists and turns, revealing the harsh realities of struggle and loss, yet ultimately celebrating the power of redemption. Through masterful storytelling, Kelly skillfully intertwines past and present, delivering a heartfelt narrative that reminds us that even in the darkest of times, there is a glimmer of hope. This captivating read will keep you engrossed until the very end, leaving you with profound reflections on life and a newfound appreciation for the journey we all embark upon. Dive into this fascinating story; it's time well spent that will leave you pondering long after you turn the final page."*
  —Skinner Myers, professor, filmmaker, scholar

*"*Killing Justice *highlights themes of misfortune brought on by an individual taken advantage of by another's greed and lack of integrity, and how blind trust without oversight can be twisted and manipulated. It expertly navigates the life of author Kelly Giles, a lawyer whose trust in a friend who commits fraud leads to him being labeled a felon too. Experiencing life from inside a cell for the first time, it perfectly encapsulates a form of controlled chaos juxtaposed to uncontrolled freedom and the back and forth between the two extremes experienced by countless others trapped in the justice system. It is an exceptional window into the mind,*

emotions, and thoughts of Mr. Giles during these trials and tribulations. How his fall from law to grace allowed him to reach higher precipices, helping him to realize the mountain he thought he was on before, was merely a mound, and how the journey is just as important as the destination."
—Andrew Sandoval, poet

"Virginia Woolf wrote, 'There are books you read, and books that read you.' Killing Justice *falls firmly into the latter category. This deeply personal journey by Kelly Giles isn't just a story; it's an experience. It resonated with my heart and soul in a way that few books ever have.*

From the very first pages, Kelly Giles' writing had me captivated. Their prose is evocative, weaving a tapestry of emotions and experiences that I found myself completely immersed in. The author's honesty and vulnerability were particularly striking. They didn't shy away from sharing their struggles and losses with a profound level of introspection to understand how and why he ended up in such a position that cost him his freedom, and which created a profound sense of connection for me as a reader.

Killing Justice *is more than just a memoir; it's a testament to the human spirit's resilience. By sharing his story, Kelly Giles has given voice to a universal experience and offered solace and strength to those who may be grappling with similar challenges. I finished the book feeling inspired and hopeful, and I know I'll carry its message with me for a long time to come.*

This book is a must-read for anyone who has ever felt lost, alone, or uncertain. It's a powerful reminder that we're not alone in our struggles, and that even in the darkest of times, there is always hope for healing and growth."
—Jacqueline Snow, transformational coach

"I enjoyed the memoir's brave, all or nothing kind of writing style with just the right amount of humor, bluntness, irony, and sarcasm. I definitely laughed a lot, had a lot of OMG moments, and also felt the pain Kelly went through during the darkest of times."
—Mimi Zhao

"Killing Justice: A Lawyer Lands in Prison and Finds his Freedom *is a poignant and thought provoking memoir that explores themes of identity, betrayal, resilience and love. Kelly's story is a testament to the human spirit's capacity to endure and overcome even the most challenging circumstances. Readers will be moved by his courage and inspired by his determination to find redemption and healing in the face of adversity."*
   —**Elizabeth Gordon, singer/songwriter**

"A daring introspective look into one man's fall into prison and his soul's climb to ultimate freedom."
   —**August Norman, author of** *the Caitlin Bergman Thrillers*

Killing Justice: A Lawyer Lands in Prison and Finds His Freedom

Copyright © 2024 by Kelly Giles

Printed in the United States of America
Hardcover ISBN: 978-1-963721-00-3
Paperback ISBN: 978-1-963721-01-0
Ebook ISBN: 978-1-963721-02-7
Library of Congress Control Number: 2024933465

Publisher's Catalog-in-Publication data
Subjects: LCSH: Giles, Kelly–Imprisonment. | Lawyers–Biography. | False arrest–Personal narratives. | Criminal justice, Administration of–United States. | Lawyers–United States–Disbarment, disqualification, etc. | Adult child abuse victims–United States–Personal narratives. | Post-traumatic stress disorder–United States–Personal narratives. | Spiritual biography. | Self-realization. | Self-actualization (Psychology) | Resilience (Personality trait) | Identity (Psychology) | LCGFT: Autobiographies. | Trial and arbitral proceedings. | BISAC: BIOGRAPHY & AUTOBIOGRAPHY / Survival. | BIOGRAPHY & AUTOBIOGRAPHY / Personal Memoirs. | LAW / Legal Profession. | LAW / Judicial Power. | LAW / Litigation. | BIOGRAPHY & AUTOBIOGRAPHY / Lawyers & Judges. | BIOGRAPHY & AUTOBIOGRAPHY / Law Enforcement. Classification: LCC: HV9950 .G55 2024 | DDC: 364.973–dc23

Desert Waves Memoirs is a division of Desert Waves Media.

Desert Waves Media
10736 Jefferson Blvd. #509
Culver City CA 90230

To Pops, who loved me better than I could love myself, and
To Mom, who loved me the best she could.

"Religion is for people who're afraid of going to hell.
Spirituality is for those who've already been there."
— Father Patrick Collins & David Bowie

"I desire mercy, not sacrifice."
— Hosea 6:6, Matthew 12: 7

"We don't see things as they are, we see them as we are."
— Anaïs Nin

"When you do things from your soul, you feel a river moving in you,
a joy. When actions come from another section, the feeling disappears.
Don't let others lead you. They may be blind or, worse, vultures."
— Rumi

"Lovers find secret places inside this violent world
where they make transactions with beauty."
— Rumi

"The Artist is no other than he who unlearns what
he has learned, in order to know himself."
— e.e. cummings

"Can you remember who you were, before the world told you who you should be?"
— Charles Bukowski

CONTENTS

THE ETERNAL OUTSIDER

I know it's hard to believe, but I remember one moment in my life more clearly than any other. My first conscious memory was finding out, at age three and a half, that not only was I adopted, but my mother was adopting another child.

We were taking a ferry boat ride to go get my baby sister, and I was out on the deck feeding a seagull when I decided to ask my mom a question.

"Why aren't we going to the hospital?"

"Because we're adopting your baby sister, just like we chose to adopt you," she gently replied.

My sister Shauna and I didn't come from Mom's tummy. But inside I wished I'd come from her tummy. I didn't want to be different.

Mom went on to say, "I picked you out. I loved you the moment I saw you. I knew that God had put you in that foster home for me, and Pops and I couldn't wait to take you home from there."

Wait, what? Was I hearing right? Not only was I adopted, but I'd also spent time in a foster home?

I remember smiling when Mom told me all this and returning to feeding the seagull. Those were curtains for the questions that were rehearsing backstage in my mind.

Why hadn't my birthmother or foster mom kept me? What was wrong with me?

I've felt like an outsider ever since. I wanted more than anything else to belong. I had no idea just how dangerous that desire to belong could be.

When my high school Careers teacher, John Clazie, and high school English teacher both had me keep a journal when I was sixteen years old, it filled a hole I didn't know I had. The freedom I found in writing those journals helped me begin to see that I never made sense to anyone, not even myself, unless I was writing. Writing was something I was able to do for myself, while almost everything else I did was for others. And this book, which I began writing as a series of letters to my younger selves, makes sense to me.

I hope it does for you too.

If not, maybe try rewriting it as a poem, and see if that helps.

CHAPTER 1

GOODBYE TO MY OLD LIFE

October 15, 2009

My old life disowns me in the fall.

It begins just like countless other days over the course of the past two decades. I meet Ling Wei, my female Chinese immigrant client in a coffee shop across the street from the Federal Building in San Francisco. The two of us chat briefly about what to expect during her green card interview, which I will accompany her to in just a few minutes' time.

"I'm so nervous about how the interview's going to go. What if he denies my case?" she asks, her hands shaking as she takes another sip of her tea.

"Take a deep breath. Just be yourself, tell the truth, and you'll be fine. Don't let the officer intimidate you. It's nothing personal; they're just doing their job. If all else fails, try pretending that they're naked," I tell her.

"And that helps?"

"Not necessarily. But it can be a lot of fun, just the same."

The interview goes smoothly, and I then go with her to her favorite local restaurant for a celebratory breakfast. Throughout our leisurely meal of blueberry pancakes swimming in maple syrup, I regale her with tales from my twenty-year career of fighting for immigrants.

I return to my hotel room after breakfast on October 15, 2009, and smile as I see the Japanese Pop art pillows I'd been too tired to notice the night before. I glance down and realize that my cellphone is still on silent mode so that the green card interview would not be interrupted. I toss my slender briefcase on the floor, kick off my shoes, and launch myself onto the bed. My head sinks back into the playful pillows as I flip on my cellphone and try to figure out just how much of a nap I might have time for before I head to the airport. Interrupting my reverie, my cellphone announces that I have two unheard messages.

The first is from my wife Linda. "Some Homeland Security agents were hammering on our door early this morning, demanding to know where you were. What's going on, Kel?" Her words slice like tiny knives through my throat. My throat feels dry as dust, and I grope for the glass of water I'd left on the bedside table.

The second is from my associate attorney Joann. "Joseph and his wife have been arrested for immigration fraud. Some storm-troopers are here now, tearing your office apart. They want your head on a stick, too." The knives in my throat have now morphed into a mini-machete, and my throat is so parched that I down the rest of the water in a single gulp. I've been working with Joseph for the past decade. This makes no sense at all. Unless Joseph has been hiding something huge. And what does his wife have to do with anything?

I try to stand, but my knees buckle, and I collapse back down onto the bed. I begin scrolling through my cellphone contacts list, searching for my civil litigator friend Tom. He is the only person I know who's had clients go through similar nightmares. My hands are trembling as I dial his office number.

"Hey, Tom," I manage to choke out, "Homeland Security agents were at our condo this morning. They've arrested Joseph and his wife May for immigration fraud. They're looking for me. What the fuck should I do?" I have no idea what Joseph might have done. And I'm even more mystified by what they could want with me.

He calmly promises to find me a criminal lawyer, and to call and tell the lead agent that I'll be flying in later that afternoon, and that my lawyer will bring me in to answer any questions they might have the next morning.

I heave my luggage into the rental car and drive distractedly down the many one-way streets between my hotel and the airport while "Head Like a Hole" by Nine Inch Nails blasts away in the background. San Francisco's "mellow vibe" from just a few hours earlier has now been replaced by a menacing vacuum.

I call Tom again from the airport. "Were you able to find me a lawyer?"

"Yeah, Kel, I found you a guy named Michael A. He's a great fighter with a huge heart, just like you."

"Thanks so much, man. Any luck getting in touch with the lead agent?"

"Not directly, but yeah, I did leave a message for him."

"What's gonna happen, Tom?"

"No idea, but hopefully they'll let Michael bring you in first thing tomorrow morning."

All I know is that my old life has started flashing before my eyes, but I still cling to the faint hope that normal programming might somehow still be restored.

Unable to imagine what fate might await me in L.A., I lose myself in the classic sci-fi novel *Ender's Game* as I fly back. My life has suddenly become so surreal that Ender's world seems far more familiar to me than my own incredibly alien planet.

When I land at LAX, instead of someone holding a sign with my name on it, I watch in horror as I see myself being suddenly surrounded by a dozen heavily armed Immigration and Customs Enforcement agents, wearing their readily identifiable POLICE ICE jackets and their ICE OFFICER badges.

They cuff me. Hard. My hands are tied together like Malcolm's had been, thirty-six years before. They tighten the iron until I wince and take me on the "perp walk" through LAX as worried faces of random strangers swim towards me. I do my best to keep from acknowledging the pain of the cuffs as they parade me out to the waiting black car.

Don't be alarmed, I want to reassure those random strangers, *you're being treated to a shining example of your tax dollars at work.* I shudder involuntarily at the cosmic irony. *If it weren't for these officers, I'd be on my way to my screenwriting class right now, to continue what I'd thought was a fictional screenplay about an adopted immigration lawyer who gets falsely accused of a crime. Now life was imitating art, which made it all the more surreal.*

Thoughts like this help distract me from the searing agony of the cuffs on my wrists. They shove me in the back of the waiting black car. I complain countless times that the cuffs are cutting off my circulation. One of the agents finally loosens them ever so slightly.

"I guess you thought you'd gotten away with it, huh?" sneers another agent.

I want to scream *"What the fuck are you talking about?"* Instead, I ask if they'd received my friend's message offering to have me come in with my lawyer the next morning. They laugh and say, "Of course we did. But what fun would it have been for us if you'd simply shown up voluntarily tomorrow morning?"

That's great. You think you're writing a fucking fictional screenplay, while they think they're the heroes of some movie, and you get to help them with their sexy trailer: "Immigration Lawyer arrested at LAX. Film at 11!"

As we continue the drive to the Metropolitan Detention Center ("MDC") downtown, the two agents joke about how much fun they had raiding my office and arresting Joseph and his wife earlier that day.

Meanwhile, I'm wishing my screenplay had stayed fictional after all.

Upon my arrival at MDC, I'm ordered by my new minder to strip, show behind my ears, bend over and cough. Once assured I'm not hiding anything, he issues me my carrot-colored jumpsuit. The guard orders me to face the rear wall as I ride up the elevator in shackles. After filling out tons of paperwork and convincing both a social worker and a doctor that I'm not about to either kill myself or die, I wait in line for the phone so that I can make my one phone call. I then call Linda and choke out "you're my rock," and weep like a baby.

Later that night, on the upper bunk of my shared cell, I toss and turn until dawn. I feel like I'm in the middle of a slow-motion car crash, and when I finally doze briefly in the pre-dawn darkness, I keep having nightmares about another car crash, the one in which Pops' old life had disowned him in the fall of 1988.

He'd been forced back out on the road as a travelling salesman when his lifelong employer, Sherwin Williams Paint in Canada, went bankrupt. The new owners, C-I-L, got rid of all of Sherwin Williams' top managers, including Pops, and an entry level job as a traveling salesman with Glidden was the only work he'd been able to find.

He'd been at that new job a little over a year when, on a business trip one day, a logging truck swerved suddenly to avoid colliding with a school bus full of children. Its load of lumber suddenly slipped free of its moorings, cascading off the back of the truck.

Pops' car was right behind the logging truck when it happened. He was buried alive. My sister and mom didn't even call me with the news until several days later, once they knew he was gonna survive. He was left with a permanent traumatic brain injury, his cognitive capacity now that of a ten-year old.

I awake with a start, my whole body shaking.

CHAPTER 2

WELCOME TO METROPOLITAN DETENTION CENTER

October 15-25, 2009

"Here's how it works: Whites stick together, Blacks and Asians stick together, or if you Mexican, you either a Southsider or Barrio Azteca, like me."

Every visible inch of Ruben, my new cellmate, is covered in elaborate tattoos, and the only hair on his head is a small, menacing goatee. He crosses his arms and casually leans against the wall with a smile I can't decipher:

"The last white guy they tried to put in a cell with me said 'Hell, no'."

"I'd be honored to share a cell with you," I reply. But something inside me rebels at what he's just said about the three groups. After all, I've spent my whole life doing what everybody else wanted me to do. The fact that I am standing in MDC Cell Block 9 is proof positive that this was not a winning strategy. Instead, I sense I am going to have to decide for myself who my true companions are going to be.

And when I tell Ruben I'd be honored to share a cell with him, there is some truth to it. I am honored he's told me about the last white guy who'd refused to share a cell with him. But I'm also relieved that he's willing to let me know upfront that he's a scary guy. On the outside, I'd too often trusted guys I only learned later were scary, like Joseph. On the inside, people seem refreshingly upfront about who they are.

Ruben then shows me where he's managed to conceal a razor blade inside our cell. I nod knowingly, while my stomach does back-flips. Is he showing me this to let me know he'll have my back if anyone tries to mess with me? Or as a warning that I'd better not piss him off?

I can't sleep. Last time I'd had insomnia had been twenty-five years earlier, when I'd blown my law school scholarship. This time I'd managed to blow up my entire career as a lawyer.

I'm still rattled by the shock of my arrest, still wincing from the pain of the recently removed cuffs, still humiliated from the bend over and cough striptease routine in front of the guard, still worried about why Ruben showed me that concealed razor blade. Yet perhaps my ultimate survival skill was that I was still in denial about how dangerous this all might be.

Not to mention the other new normals. Like how tiny the eight by ten cell is that I find myself sharing with Ruben, just in case I'd forgotten how luxurious my hotel room of just a few hours earlier had been. Or like being locked down all night, with no spacious hotel bathroom to relieve myself in. No, this was a real prison all right. With an open shithole for Ruben and me to share. Sure, I'd had no problem with outhouses on camping trips or beach visits or music festivals. But I've never shared a shithole before, let alone with a scary dude like Ruben.

Had he told me that story about the last white guy refusing to share a cell with him and showed me that concealed razor blade as a warning? So that if he killed me in my sleep, at least he'd given me the option to relocate beforehand? I grab a Bible from the prison library before the guards lock us down for the night, so I have something to read in bed. Who knows? Maybe if I do manage to fall asleep and Ruben tries to slash me in my bunk, he'll slice the Bible instead, and I'll miraculously live to tell the tale.

How had I ended up here? Had Joseph, my friend of twenty years who I'd been of counsel to for the past decade, been lying to me when he'd said the Feds were investigating him about federal crimes he'd been falsely accused of? Had I been lying to myself to have believed him so readily?

As I climb into my hard, uncomfortable upper bunk with a wafer-thin mattress, I start obsessively re-reading the book of Job. I figure if he could make it all through all his sufferings without simply taking his wife's advice to "curse God and die", maybe I could, too.

Now while re-reading Job might not seem to be the best idea for a bedtime story, there is no way I am going to be able to sleep tonight anyway. My sleeplessness stems from the same deep fear that had haunted me a quarter century earlier, that nobody could ever possibly love me now. Disappointing my god-like adoptive mom Pat had tormented me then. It torments me now. As dawn approaches, however, it suddenly strikes me that I've believed for far too long that my initials, KEDG, had to stand for "Kelly Entirely Dependent upon Goodness" for me to be worthy of love. An image of my foster mom Grace suddenly flashes through my mind, and I begin trembling with the dawning awareness that my initials stand for "Kelly Entirely Dependent upon Grace." It will be years before the difference between goodness and grace slowly begins to become clearer to me, but at least a crack has now opened in my prison of fear.

After my sleepless night, I learn the hard way that you gotta hustle if you're going to get any food. I'm last in line for breakfast, and so all I manage to get is a bowl of dry cereal, missing out on a spoon or any milk. I sit down on a plastic bench in a sleep-deprived daze, and before I have a chance to wonder how I'll choke down my dry Special K, a group of white guys sit down around me.

"Welcome to the breakfast club," they say.

One of them offers me some milk, another one a spoon, and a third one an orange. I'm part of the Whitey gang. Just like that. Apparently, they are telling me in no uncertain terms, they are to be my new companions here. Just like Ruben had said. Too exhausted to say no, I simply accept their offerings and polish off my meal so I can get ready for my bond hearing, where a judge will decide if I should be denied bond, in which case I will have to remain in prison until after my trial, or if I will be allowed to be released on bond, and if so, how much the bond will be. I had gotten used to playing the role of a lawyer. But what's expected of me now? Who am I supposed to be? Where do I belong? Way back when I was in the third grade, almost forty years ago, and growing up in Victoria, Canada, which was also known as "the whitest part of Whitelandia," I'd written a letter to the editor of the *Victoria Times-Colonist* expressing my opinion that "integration is a wonderful thing, as we can learn so much from other cultures," which miraculously got published. What did I know about other cultures growing up? All I knew was that being adopted made me feel as if I was from "another culture." Since Pops, my adoptive dad, had nicknamed me "Special K", I felt like being from another culture must be a good thing.

I try to hold on to the memory of the small kindness of the milk and spoon and orange, because the rest of the day is a catalogue of small humiliations.

I'm allowed to wear my own clothes - the black sweats, the ONE t-shirt, and the white Reeboks I'd been arrested in - to go to the Roybal Federal Courthouse. But getting them involves being forced to strip naked in front of a female ICE agent, changing in front of her, and then being escorted in handcuffs to the holding area where I wait like a cow in a pen until it is time to be handed over to the U.S. Marshalls. They take my shoelaces, then photograph and fingerprint me. Afterwards I'm shuffled into a fear and sweat-drenched cell with a dozen other detainees and tossed a bag lunch consisting of a stale crust of bread and a slimy slice of bologna, which makes me yearn for the maple syrup-drenched pancakes I'd been feasting on just a day earlier. Several hours later I'm shunted out to an interview with a pre-trial services officer. Will I be granted bond? Or will my request be denied, as most are, and will I be forced to fight my case from behind bars?

"Hello, Mr. Giles. I realize your lawyer's not here yet, but I've got to go into court in a few minutes. Unless you're willing to talk to me without your lawyer present, the government lawyer's going to claim that you're a flight risk and so should be denied bond, and I'll have no way of responding on your behalf," she begins.

"Well, then, I guess I'd better talk to you."

"Okay, sir, how much money did you make last year?"

"Sixty grand."

"Seriously, that's it? And how long have you been a lawyer?"

"Seriously, that's it. Twenty years."

"Wow. Given how little you made last year, I'm going to ask the judge to set your bond at around twenty grand."

"Okay, thanks so much!" I said, and truly meant it. Federal bonds could be set astronomically high.

"No problem. See you in court."

Then back to the cell for more hours of waiting, this time cuffed hand and foot. I feel so alone, despite being surrounded by other inmates. After lingering a while longer, we're finally taken to a holding area on the side of the courtroom where we wait several more hours for all the pre-trial reports to come in. I watch lawyers come in and out of the room. Why am I one of the detainees and no longer one of them?

The judge finally enters the courtroom, at which time family and friends are allowed to enter. I'm thrilled to see Linda, but it is heartbreaking to see her staring off into the distance, not once looking my way. I will learn later that the bailiff has ordered her not to make eye contact with me, so I must be content just to look at her lovely, familiar face.

About an hour later, I see a private lawyer arrive, and go over to the public defender, Susan, and ask for a file. He then spends several minutes reviewing it, talks with Linda for several more minutes, at which point I realize he must be Michael A., the lawyer Tom had hired for me, and finally makes his way over to me.

"So, are you going to fight for bond for me? The public defender said I didn't have a prayer," I say.

"Well, she may have a point. The Assistant District Counsel is going to say that you've been accused of serious crimes and that you're a major flight risk, as you have no real ties to keep you here."

"Well, try telling them this. First, I'm not guilty of anything. Second, despite their raid on my office, I have two detained clients with bond hearings next week who need me to fight for them. And finally, that I love Linda deeply, and that she has major health issues."

"I'll give it my best shot."

I look around at my fellow inmates. There are thirteen of us. The other twelve are all African American. They are all represented by the same Hispanic female public defender.

Each time one of their names is called, I watch that clearly over-whelmed young woman rise to her feet and beg the judge for mercy on their behalf.

Each time the response is the same: "Request for bond denied."

Each time I hear those words, my throat tightens.

Can this judge ever be persuaded to agree to a bond for any of us?

After the twelve other bond requests have all been denied, my case is the last to be called.

"Please state your name for the record," the judge begins.

"Kelly Giles, your Honor."

"And what is the government's position?"

"Mr. Giles is a dangerous criminal, charged with two felonies, Conspiracy to Commit Immigration Fraud and Obstruction of Justice, and is a major flight risk, as he is a dual U.S./Canadian citizen who has travelled to both Canada and China several times within the past six months. We have raided his office, pretty much shutting his operation down, so he has no viable means of supporting himself, nor does he have any real ties here."

"And what is your position, defense counsel?"

"Talk about night and day, your Honor. Innocent until proven guilty used to be a hallmark of our judicial system, but the government seems to now find that concept archaic. Despite his office having been raided, several of his detained immigrant clients are counting on Kelly to fight for their release on bond in immigration court next week. In addition, he and Linda have been married for almost twenty years, and she has fibromyalgia and multiple chemical sensitivity. Kelly would never con-sider fleeing, as he is desperately needed by both Linda and his clients."

"We also had to arrest Mr. Giles at LAX to prevent him from fleeing," answers the Assistant District Counsel Kevin.

"Far from it! His friend Tom had informed the government that Kelly would be turning himself in this morning, and they simply chose not to believe him. He was returning from his client's green card interview in San Francisco, and so was clearly not 'fleeing' anywhere," counters Michael.

The Judge then announces his decision.

"Okay, having carefully considered both side's arguments, I am setting Mr. Giles' bond at two hundred fifty thousand dollars. He is not to leave the Central District of California, nor go to any airport or bus terminal without the consent of Pre-Trial Services. His next hearing is set for November 2nd, and since it is now after five pm, he shall remain detained until his bond can be posted."

My heart can't sit still. A ripple of relief that I've been granted bond. A tsunami of terror that we can't afford it. I will later learn that my bond had been based on Joseph's bond, but Joseph's mansion worth a million and a half would make a quarter of a million - dollar bond for both himself and his wife easily makeable. Our little condo we got for a little over a hundred grand? Not so much. Would I be forced to fight my case from a prison cell?

"I'll come see you on Sunday!" Michael calls out to me as they're taking me away, bound hand and feet.

* * * * *

Now back in my white coveralls and white canvas sneakers, I'm once again handed a bag lunch, having once more arrived at my cell block too late for dinner.

As I stare out through the bars of our prison cellblock at the lights of the city, still shaken by the bond amount, I try to find something to take comfort in. One of my greatest fears, ever since that day when Joseph told me he was being investigated by the Feds – that one day I might end up behind bars – has been realized, and I haven't fallen apart completely. I had repressed these fears, however, as it had made much more sense to believe instead that Joseph had been falsely accused, as he had claimed at the time. Two of my long-held illusions have finally been shattered: that life is fair, and that I can control my life. I stop feeling sorry for myself for a moment. Instead, I feel sorry for all those people outside these prison walls, still trapped within their invisible prisons of fear. I'd been in that prison myself for at least a decade, afraid of doing anything that might upset Joseph for fear he might abandon me. Instead, I'd abandoned myself.

The next morning, after having finally gotten some sleep, I end up last in line for breakfast once again, missing out yet again on both milk and a spoon. This time, however, I head straight over to a table full of Black inmates, who I feel are my true companions here. I have just been screwed over, but they've spent much of their lives being screwed over. "Welcome to the Hood," they joke, but one of them offers me milk, and another offers me a spoon for my cereal.

Shortly after eating lunch, once again at the Black inmate table, I sign up for and get in line to attend a religious service. While waiting in line, the white shot-caller, Walter, gets in my face and warns, "We haven't been seeing you around lately, Giles."

Before I can say a word, from behind me comes the voice of Terrell, the Black shot-caller, saying, "He's with us."

After having spent the past decade eating bread with someone I believed was a true companion named Joseph, it seems I have finally found my way to my actual true companions.

On Sunday afternoon, after I've eaten five straight meals over the past day and a half with the Black inmates, and right before I'm about to go meet with my lawyer, Walter comes into my cell and sits down.

"So do you like the Blacks?" he begins.

"I got no problem with them, why?"

"Well, just to be clear, I'm no racist. There are a few skinheads and Aryan Brotherhood types around, so be thankful that I'm in charge, and not them."

"Your point being–?"

"Now, none of the Black inmates has complained to me just yet, but I noticed today at lunch that a few of them were standing around, as you were sitting at their table, leaving them with nowhere to sit. In the interest of keeping the peace, you might want to consider sitting somewhere else."

"All right, I'll keep that in mind."

While waiting in the corridor to go meet with my lawyer a few minutes later, I notice Terrell at the far end of the hallway.

"Hey, Terrell, if there's not enough seats at the table for all of you, just let me know, as Walter just warned me that it could be a problem," I begin.

"That's bullshit, Kel! You're accepted, plain and simple. Walter's just trying to play politics. Don't worry about it."

"Ok, cool, thanks!"

Returning from my attorney visit too late for dinner, I'm thrilled to discover that my unit's Chief Officer, or "CO", has saved a dinner tray for me. Once I finish polishing off my dinner at Terrell's table, I suddenly find myself getting a chance to enjoy the "politics" of my situation.

Terrell immediately offers me a much more appetizing, specially-prepared version of the main course. I then strike up a conversation with Yoshi, who's reading *The First Circle* by Solzhenitsyn, one of my favorite authors. While Yoshi and I carry on an animated conversation, Walter, trying desperately not to be outdone by Terrell, hands me a pen, some writing paper, and an envelope.

Then, not to be outdone by either Walter or Terrell, Yoshi gives me some additional pens, several more pages of writing paper, numerous envelopes and stamps, two books to read, several teabags, a bag of oatmeal cookies, and a bottle of shampoo.

The highlight of the day's events, however, comes when Yoshi's Latino roommate Gustavo offers me a massive piece of the most delicious fresh-baked apple crisp I've ever eaten.

* * * * *

That Friday evening, I'm on the phone with Linda. She's been fighting like hell all week to get my bond posted, as, thank God, our condo has appreciated just enough in value to enable her to do so. If I don't get out tonight, I won't be getting out until Monday.

"God, I miss you, dear. I hope you managed to get some sleep this week. Did they say if I might be getting out tonight?" I ask her, my hands trembling.

"No one knows. The Assistant District Counsel, after some prodding by Michael, finally said the papers were in order, but it'd be up to the prison. What are they telling you?"

"Just that I'll know by nine pm....Wait, wait, the CO is giving me the thumbs up...I'm getting the fuck out of here! See you soon!"

"Good luck!" the Chief Officer says. "And remember, you were only a detainee, never a convict!"

I'm mobbed by my fellow inmates as news begins to spread of my imminent release. The Mexican inmates leave their contact info with me, in case they need any immigration help in future. The rest of my fellow inmates divide up my clothes and other prison belongings among themselves. Finally, one of my white fellow inmates comes up to me and quietly says, "Thanks so much for standing up to Walter like you did this week."

A guard escorts me back down the elevator to the loading dock. This time I am allowed to face him.

"So when you comin' back here?" he asks.

"In two weeks, for my next hearing," I say.

"Wrong. You're supposed to say, 'Never!'"

"Got it. From your lips to God's ears."

* * * * *

Now back in my street-clothes, I am escorted to the elevator, and then released at the corner of Temple and Alameda. Bizarrely, Joseph, who'd been in a different cellblock from me, is released along with me, as is a third inmate, a stranger to us both, who seems to be hanging on our every word, hoping we might say something about our case.

Instead, Joseph simply says to me, "I'm fully responsible for what happened, and I will take full responsibility for it. You've got to admit, though, this is a great opportunity for you to find a new career."

I feel betrayed. Shocked. Too stunned to respond, I simply watch him walk briskly away. Linda will later tell me that Joseph's wife, May, told her much the same thing when they were down at the bond office, that I would be fine, as I had had nothing to do with what Joseph had done. I look around, a little disoriented, and silently curse myself for not having found out where exactly I'd be released so I could have let Linda know.

Before going in search of her, however, I struggle to reinsert my now broken-beyond-repair shoelaces back into my running shoes, failing miserably. Then I wander up Alameda towards Aliso and the Metropolitan Detention Center.

My heart rockets skyward when I see Linda with her dark brown eyes wet with tears, sitting on the steps between the federal courthouse and the MDC. I race over and we embrace for the longest time, and weep, and weep, and weep.

Just forty-eight hours later, that Sunday evening at the Rose Bowl, as U2 plays "Walk On" in front of around a hundred thousand rapturous fans, Linda and I and our fellow Amnesty International volunteers slowly "walk on" to the stage, holding masks of Aung San Suu Kyi in front of our faces.

From the prison I'd been released from just forty-eight hours earlier, I now proudly take the stage on behalf of a wrongfully detained individual, who'd been under house arrest in Burma for most of the twenty years I had spent as an immigration lawyer.

The concert is the first ever to be broadcast live worldwide on YouTube, and I desperately hope that it will help finally bring an end to her prolonged unlawful detention. On November 23, 2010, just over one year later, that becomes a reality.

That night, I can't really sleep. I think about how someone else had once suggested I might want to consider another career, like Joseph had now done. At sixteen I'd told my mom I'd wanted to be a hotel manager, but she'd dismissed it. So I'd buried my desires, gone to college and majored in business to make mom happy, and become a lawyer to make mom happy. And now I may be about to lose all that.

CHAPTER 3

MEETING WITH MICHAEL AT MDC

October 18, 2009

Lawyer is Accused of Selling Fake Work Visas screamed the *LA Times* head-line. My newly-retained criminal lawyer, Michael A, showed this to me as we sat across from each in the Metropolitan Detention Center, or "MDC", visiting area. Only Michael had seen the indictment at this point, so I had no idea what I was being accused of.

"Aside from spelling my middle names, Einstein and Darwin, right, and getting my age and the fact that I was arrested at LAX upon 'return-ing' from a trip right, everything else this article says about me is a lie. Did anyone even bother to contact you before they ran this bullshit story?"

"Yeah, one reporter did, and I told him that you had been wrongfully accused. I guess that wasn't newsworthy enough for them, though. Your middle name Einstein, however, has certainly been getting you lots of attention."

"How so?"

Michael laughed. "Well, the response to the article that seems to have gone viral is 'For this guy it seems like everything is relative.'"

"Oh great, so now I'm both a perp and a punch line."

Michael laughed again. "Yeah, but it could be worse."

"Really?"

"Sure, you could have actually done the things they're accusing you of, as then we'd have no case."

I lifted my eyes from the floor to meet his gaze.

"So you believe that I've been wrongfully accused, then?"

"Well, your friend Tom, who contacted me to represent you, is a good friend of mine. And since he speaks so highly of your character, unless the documents prove otherwise, I have no reason to doubt you.

I expect there'll be a ton of documents they'll be dumping on us in discovery soon to try to back up their accusations. Once I review the record, I'll have a better sense of what the prosecutor has, and what we're up against."

"So how much is this going to cost me?

I gazed downwards once again, thinking about how I couldn't possibly afford this guy.

"Yeah, you're not my typical fat-cat, guilty-as-hell career criminal, like the drug lord I recently got a hell of a plea deal for. If I were to charge you my regular rate, given the volume of documents they're almost certain to be dumping on us soon, and given how long I will probably have to spend fighting this case, my best guess would be eighty to a hundred grand, assuming we can get them to agree to a reasonable plea. It would go even higher than that if we need to go to trial, though."

I shifted uneasily in my chair.

"Wow. I couldn't even come close to being able to afford even the low end of that range."

"Well, like I said, I'd find it refreshing to fight for a wrongfully accused client for a change. So how much do you think you might be able to afford?"

Lifting my gaze to his once again, I replied, "Twenty grand, tops."

Without blinking, he immediately answered. "Okay, I'll find a way to make that work. Hopefully we'll be able to convince them to agree to a plea that will enable you to both keep your law license and not have to spend any more time in the slammer once you manage to get bonded out of here."

"Thanks so much, Michael. I hope to God you're able to pull that off."

I didn't like thinking of myself as Felon Kel. I dove deep to bring up another two versions of me that I thought might help: Smart Kel, which had protected me from the world, and Lawyer Kel, which had cemented my place in it.

CHAPTER 4

THE RISE AND FALL OF SMART KEL

1970-1984

It was the fall of 1970, and I was seven years old. Mom had been reading to me since she and Pops adopted me six years earlier. I had impressed the hell out of my kindergarten teacher, Mrs. Springer, by already knowing how to sound out words.

I had breezed through first grade at Seaview Elementary. Life outside of school was way more interesting than life at school. We had this neighbor, whose name was Helen Woods, who used to walk around barefoot all the time. I wanted to be as free and fearless as her when I grew up. My sister felt otherwise. She kept saying to me, "Mom would never let such dirty feet inside the house!"

Now I was starting second grade. Wait, let me rephrase that: now I was finishing second grade. It had only been a month, and I had already finished the year's work.

I started reading all the *Children's Digests* I could lay my hands on. This soon convinced the powers that be at Seaview Elementary School in Port Moody to move me into the third grade.

Everything was going great until Pop got a promotion in December, and suddenly we were leaving Port Moody on the lower mainland and taking yet another ferry boat ride, just like the one we'd taken three and a half years earlier to go get my baby sister, over to Vancouver Island.

This time, though, instead of going to Comox, where we got my sister, we went to Victoria.

It was now January of 1971, and my new school, Glanford Elementary, didn't believe in putting kids ahead, so back to the second grade I went. I had learned to write cursive during my brief visit to the third grade, and so I started writing out all my homework assignments in cursive, rather than block printing like my classmates. My second-grade teacher soon tired of this routine and locked me in a room and gave me a bunch of tests to take. The next day I was rewarded by being allowed to finish the year in the third grade. Smart Kel had arrived to help me feel like I belonged.

My need to be the best at everything, to feel like I belonged despite my having been adopted, would drive me to be on the honor roll all through elementary, junior high and high school, to be runner up for valedictorian at my undergrad despite hating my major, and to get a perfect score on my LSAT. It would also set me up for a hell of a shock when I arrived at Pepperdine for my first semester of law school.

Adoptees are known for trying to overcompensate for having been adopted with delusions of grandeur, but hey, John Lennon, Eric Clapton, and Steve Jobs were adoptees who dreamed big. I was gonna cruise through law school, and then figure out how to save the world as a lawyer. What could possibly go wrong?

It was the first week of October, 1984. A crowd had gathered in front of the wall next to the lockers on the lower level of Pepperdine Law School. Our first set of grades as first year law students were there for all to see.

I'd been overwhelmed by the sheer volume of work that first month. My little undergrad, Trinity Western University, where I'd been runner up for valedictorian, had been smaller than my high school.

The perfect score on my LSAT now felt like a distant memory.

Suddenly I'd found myself 1,700 miles from home. No more ferry boat rides on weekends for some home-cooked meals or to get my laundry done.

I was here on a student visa, and so without my green card I couldn't get financial aid. My scholarship only covered tuition, and Malibu was hella expensive. I asked the Canadian government, who'd helped me out during my undergrad years, for a six-thousand-dollar loan, and they'd sent me six hundred.

My parents had rented my room out and had just sent me the first rent check, so I could stock up on Kraft Mac & Cheese for the month to come.

To renew my scholarship, I would need to stay in the top ten percent. No problem, I thought to myself, that runner-up for valedictorian and perfect score on my LSAT hadn't been all that long ago, had they?

No matter how overwhelming that first month had seemed, of course I was still gonna end up at or near the top ten percent, right?

Right?

After the crowd had mostly wandered off, I crept cautiously up to the wall, hoping against hope my worst fears about how that first month had gone would not be realized. It took a while to finally find my name, and when I did, I didn't recognize it.

No, no, no, no, no. That couldn't possibly be me. I'm a Gemini, after all. It must be my evil twin, playing a cruel trick on me.

Bottom half. Not even a hope in hell that I could ever possibly crawl back up to the top ten percent and renew my scholarship and be back next fall.

My life was over. My whole life I'd had to be the best, or I was nobody. Now I was the worst.

Now that my fear of disappointing mom had reached Red Alert levels, I thrashed around for some way to survive the semester.

I couldn't sleep. One flurazepam per night seemed to suffice for the first month. By the second month, it was up to two. By months three and four, I was popping three or four sleeping pills a night just to get an hour or two of sleep. I'd managed to stockpile plenty after repeated trips to the campus health clinic. I was still attending classes, but I was hanging by a thread.

I began writing obsessively, something I had begun doing when I was seven years old and had always loved. Writing was the only way I knew to try to contain the chaos that was consuming me, and so I called my memoir *Roadmaps Through Hell*, scarcely imagining that the hell I was chronicling then would be dwarfed by a far deeper hell twenty-five years later. With the death of my Smart Kel mind which had sustained me since the age of seven, my Writer Kel heart and soul had to rush into the breach to prevent me from falling apart completely.

When I flew home that Christmas, I was terrified that I might never sleep again and/or be hopelessly addicted to sleeping pills. Pops crept in quietly as I lay in the roll-away bed in the rec room, and gently whispered, "Take a deep breath." I slept for fourteen hours. My chaotic heart had finally found the unconditional love it had been longing for. I was Pops' beloved son. I belonged.

CHAPTER 5

SHIPPING OUT TO TAFTGHANISTAN

April 29-May 18, 2013

Judge Wu had issued me my orders. I was to self-surrender to Taft Federal Prison no later than noon on Monday, April 29, 2013, to begin serving my ten-month sentence. My lawyer, Michael, had informed me that it was a privilege to be allowed to self-surrender, but I certainly wasn't feeling very privileged as my departure date drew near. Terrified? Yes. Privileged? Hell no.

My friend Jason had hoped to be able to drive Linda and me to up to Taft that day. He was hoping to shoot some footage for the documentary project we'd been working on for the past several months, and I needed him to drive so that Linda would not be forced to make the long drive back herself.

At the last minute, however, one of Jason's classes had been rescheduled to April 29th, and we were forced to scramble to try and come up with an eleventh hour replacement for him. So on Sunday, April 28th, 2013, on the eve of my self-surrender date, I went to church in search of Jason's replacement. Fortunately, Larry, a husky, beautifully tatted friend from my home church group, who'd done time in prison himself, volunteered his services as our chauffeur.

Since I'd been unable to file my request for a certificate of non-operational status for my car online with the Department of Motor Vehicles, as soon as Larry picked us up the next morning in his battered white pickup truck, we headed over to the DMV in Culver City to file in person. That way we could at least cancel my car insurance while I was going to be away. I sweated it out as the line inched slowly forward, praying that we wouldn't hit too much traffic on our way up to Taft so that I would make it in time for my noon deadline. When I finally made it to the front of the line and got everything filed, I raced out and hopped in the truck and off we went.

On the Friday before, I'd requested a one-year leave of absence from my practice as a Registered Canadian Immigration Consultant. Thank God that I'd applied for, and obtained, a license to practice Canadian immigration law as a registered consultant several years earlier, as several of Joseph's clients had needed my help to immigrate to Canada rather than the U.S. So even though I'd lost my California Bar license and could no longer practice U.S. immigration law, my Canadian license remained valid.

The basis for my leave of absence request was that I needed a sabbatical to recover from my recent diagnosis of Post-Traumatic Stress Disorder.

And finally, several of my "Art of Creative Nonfiction" classmates from the UCLA Extension class I'd just wrapped up had gently chided me that they were jealous of my being able to go on such an extended writer's retreat. There was some basis to this, as I'd read that two of the favorite locations for writers are lighthouses and prisons. I just wished I was on my way to a lighthouse instead.

Looking back on my life up until that point, it seemed as though my life had been consumed by chaos. Now, however much I might have avoided stillness before, I had been sentenced to it.

So as Larry, Linda and I crawled up the 405 and then the 5 freeways on our way to Taftghanistan (as I felt like I was going to war), I kept requesting all my favorite songs on Larry's iPod. I sang along at the top of my lungs, desperately trying to make the most of my final few hours of freedom. I had fought back the fear as best I could. I was wearing my black and white "The Dude Abides" *Big Lebowski* t-shirt which Larry and his wife had bought me as a going away present, to try and show how nonchalant I was about this day, but inside I was a frightened little boy. As I started getting ready to turn over my cellphone and the rest of my meager possessions to Linda for safekeeping, I received one final text from my good friend Olivia, whose "I'll be praying for you" meant the world to me in that dread-filled vehicle.

Fortunately, traffic was light on both the 405 and 5 as we headed north from Los Angeles to Taft, so we had time to stop at the In-N-Out Burger in Valencia for my late morning "last meal" before my farewell to freedom was finalized. Oh, the countless times over the next several months that I would look back with longing at the memory of such divine dining that day.

As we arrived in Taftghanistan and clambered out of Larry's pickup, Larry continued to film some documentary footage for Jason as we made our way over to the entrance.

"Put that fucking camera away!" shouted one of the prison officials.

Larry dutifully complied.

Having read a *Preparing for Prison* e-book recently, I was worried that I might be forced to pay to have my street clothes shipped home for me. But as I was preparing to strip out of my "Dude Abides" t-shirt, the prison guard who I was about to surrender myself to said they would mail my clothes home for me for free. One small blessing to be grateful for, I suppose.

I gave Larry a quick hug. Linda and I tearfully embraced. I waved mournfully back to them as they slowly departed and headed in to begin my self-surrender ritual. Because the arrival area at Taft is part of the medium security facility which houses immigrant detainees, after I stripped out of my street clothes, I had to don a pumpkin-colored jumpsuit and be shackled until someone could be found to escort me from there over to the minimum-security camp.

"Hopefully this is the last time you'll need to be shackled like this while you're here," one of the guards said sympathetically.

As I lay back on a concrete slab in the dingy cell and stared blindly at the yellowing ceiling, the reality of my situation slowly began sinking in. *Fuck*, I thought to myself. *How did it ever come to this? What I wouldn't give to be driving back to Culver City with Linda and Larry right now. My life is over.*

Eventually, one of the guards casually asked me how I'd ended up there.

"I got fucked over by a friend," I replied.

"Sure, man," he laughed, "nobody's ever guilty around here."

Finally, however, I was given my first medical exam by a tall, beautiful brunette nurse named Janine. She made me feel fully human, rather than just another dirtbag inmate. She listened sympathetically to my story. "Don't let them break your spirit!" she said. She seemed to be one of the precious few prison staff who had held on to her humanity in that heartless bureaucracy.

I finally got done being taunted by the mostly cynical guards, and soothed by the sympathetic nurse, and was escorted over to the entrance to the minimum-security camp at Taft Federal Prison. There I was unshackled and allowed to change into khakis and a white t-shirt and handed a mattress.

The guard who was escorting me introduced me to Leo, a tall, lanky Black inmate. "Leo's in your dorm, and will help show you around."

I laid my wafer-thin mattress down and shook Leo's hand. "Good to meet you, Leo."

"Great to meet you too, Kel. We're in Dorm C, down at the far end of the compound, on the upper level. Let's head over there now so you can start getting settled."

Leo took me over to the chapel first, though. "Here's some toiletries to get you started, Kel. The guys in chapel donate some of their commissary items every week to help the new guys like yourself out."

"Wow, that's great. Thanks!"

Just then Joseph appeared. "Hey, Kel, so great to see you. Since we're going to be together here these next few months, we should try to help each other out in any way we can."

Fuck that shit! What the hell were they thinking, sending us both here? I'm really going to have to work on my anger management these next few months. Look where all your help landed me, dude!

I clenched and unclenched my fists, faking a smile, while Joseph chattered away.

The three of us climbed the stairs up to C Dorm, and Leo pointed me to a three-man cube across from his. There was a two-man bunk bed on the left, and a single bed on the right.

"Go ahead and put your mattress on that upper bunk. I'll be right back," Leo said, and drifted over to his own cube for a moment.

"Look, Kel, that single bed in your cube has no mattress on it. You should put your mattress there instead," suggested Joseph.

"Yeah, sure, maybe," I mumbled, and tried to look busy until Joseph finally took the hint and wandered off.

Leo came back to my cube and I asked him about Joseph's suggestion.

"Good thing you didn't take his advice, Kel," Leo replied, "as that would have got your ass sent to the hole."

Though it may sound bizarre to say this, prison felt far safer to me than almost anywhere I'd ever been before. As a former foster child, I had always felt safer in institutions than in anything remotely resembling a family. I had only ever had glimpses of what home was supposed to feel like.

Prison did seem safer than most anywhere else I'd been. Prison also stripped away all the distractions of the outside world and forced me to focus on the things that mattered most to me, reading and writing.

But most of what I wrote now was shit. I couldn't deal with the reality of where I'd ended up. So I wrote a lot of long-winded rants about why I didn't deserve to be there. Or about how heroically I was spending my time there.

Bullshit.

I was no fucking hero.

I was a scared little kid.

I'd been a scared little kid my whole life. I had loved working with Joseph at first because he felt like a father figure, and I could keep being that little boy I'd always been. And even if it was a totally fucked-up home, I couldn't tell the difference, because if all felt so familiar. I had never, ever been good enough for my adoptive mom, and I would never, ever be good enough for Joseph. He even made me pay him nearly a quarter of a million dollars over a two-year period for the privilege of feeling like I'd finally found a home. But more about that later.

So maybe I really did, if not deserve, at least need to go to prison after all, if only to force me to finally open my eyes to the way the world really works, and to hopefully, finally, grow the fuck up.

What they don't tell you about federal prison camp is that there's an e-book called *Lessons from Prison*. I had asked my pre-trial services officer what prison was going to be like and had been sent a link to that helpful title.

Another thing they don't tell you, which I learned from that e-book, is that you'd better find a friend with a full tank of gas to take you there. Had I failed to do so, and instead decided to try to save a little money on gas by self-surrendering at the local Federal Marshal's office in Los Angeles, they would have taken me to prison. Just not the prison I had been sentenced to, which was Taft. Instead, they would have taken me to whichever prison the next Federal Marshal's bus happened to be going to. I'd have been shackled, as it probably would not have been going to a minimum-security camp like Taft. I may have ended up in Nevada. Or New Mexico. It may have taken months before I finally ended up at Taft.

Another thing they don't tell you about federal prison camp, specifically, is that there are no prison gates. Or even walls. As I entered the minimum-security camp, I kept looking for the guard tower they would try to shoot me from if I tried to escape. Like the one at Manzanar, where my father-in-law had been imprisoned during the Second World War. Instead, I was free to leave, as long as I was willing to risk heat stroke trying to make a break for it through the California desert.

The next thing they don't tell you is that they feed you for twenty-five cents a day. That's a hell of a lot of rice and beans. And a brilliant business model.

Another thing they don't tell you is that they make you work for twelve cents an hour. *Didn't the Thirteenth Amendment abolish slavery?* I remember asking myself when informed of this requirement. "Except in cases of punishment for crime" was the helpful answer I found when re-reading the Thirteenth Amendment in the prison library one day, just for fun.

The next thing they don't tell you is that if you want to eat anything that's not on the twenty-five cents a day chow hall menu, you must buy it in commissary. Anything healthy, like tuna. Or anything delicious, like Häagen-Dazs white chocolate raspberry truffle ice cream.

Another thing they don't tell you is that you must take fun classes like "Foods and Nutrition". In that class you learn about the ten food items most likely to kill you. That nine of the ten are the best-selling items in commissary. And that at the top of that list is my personal favorite dessert of death, the above-mentioned Häagen-Dazs.

The last thing they don't tell you is that Häagen-Dazs ice cream costs four dollars and eighty cents in commissary. Which means a week's worth of work at twelve cents an hour. But so worth it. If I couldn't experience the joy of dying in a hail of bullets while trying to escape, I wanted my epitaph at least to read, "He died of an overdose of Häagen-Dazs white chocolate raspberry truffle ice cream."

God, I'm starving. I'd self-surrendered just before noon, but by the time Leo had helped escort me to my new home in dorm C, dinner, which was served at 4:30 each day, was long over.

This minimum-security camp called cell-blocks dorms, and cells were called cubes. This renaming, however, simply made my monochrome surroundings that much more depressing.

I lay down on my ultra-thin mattress, hoping my hunger pangs would subside, and stared up at the coffin-grey ceiling.

Just then Leo popped his head inside my cube. "How'd you like a tuna sandwich?" he asked, handing me that, along with a small bag of chips, a Snickers bar, and a tattered white baseball cap.

"I'd love one, thanks!" I savored the sandwich, chips, and chocolate bar, reminding myself there would be no fridge for me to raid if I got hungry later.

As I was doing so, Floyd, a burly Black guy from the cube next to mine, introduced himself. "I'm in the sixteenth year of an eighteen-year sentence," he began. "This place is my reward for good behavior at some of my earlier stops on the federal prison expressway. Where's the rest of your bedding?" he asked, glancing at my meager mattress.

"That's all they gave me," I replied.

"I'll be right back." He headed off down the corridor between the two upper dorms, C and D, and returned a few minutes later with a pillow and the rest of my bedding, along with an extra sheet for good measure. "Do you know how to make a military style bed?" he asked.

"Hell, no," I answered. "I had a tough enough time making my bed well enough to satisfy my mom when I was a kid."

"Well, watch and learn, son," he said. I climbed down from my upper bunk, and watched in awe as Floyd expertly made my bed. He then handed me the extra sheet, saying, "You know the drill," and, for once, I did. I'd learned from reading *Orange is the New Black* that the easiest way to pass early morning inspections was simply to sleep under an extra sheet on top of a freshly made bed, so that was exactly what I would do.

I had drained virtually all my meager savings and borrowed heavily from Linda to fight my case for the past three years. The lawyer had cost twenty grand, and the expert witness another ten grand. That had left me with barely three grand to my name. This whopping sum I had withdrawn in its entirety and brought with me in cash so that I would at least have something in my commissary account with which to clothe and feed myself.

On my first morning after I had self-surrendered, I went down to the dorm resident administrator's office to check the balance in my commissary account and found that it was zero. I checked again the next morning, and the next, and the next, and for an entire week the balance remained the same.

Each day's zero balance brought with it a deepening sense of desperation, as each new inmate is only issued a bare minimum of clothing. One pair of socks, one pair of underwear, one pair of grey khakis, and one grey t-shirt. Oh, yeah, and one pair of flimsy flip-flops.

So it came as a huge relief when one of my dorm-mates kicked me over a beat-up pair of running shoes on day two, and when another handed me a slightly torn, but wearable pair of shorts on my way back from the restroom on day four, and when yet another tossed a white tee-shirt into my cube on day six.

Even Joseph, who was responsible for my being here, got in on the act, giving me a couple of bowls, a tumbler, and a plastic cutlery set. I held up the utensils. In federal prison, just as on the outside, I could expect nothing but the best from Joseph.

I had never felt more alone. Being surrounded by five hundred other souls only made the feeling worse, as there was no one I dared bare my soul to. I submitted both my phone and email lists to our dorm's resident administrator, who served as liaison between the prison staff and us inmates, the day after I arrived. I then followed up with him the next day to see if it had been approved. "Not yet," he replied. And the next day, same thing. And the next. And the next. Finally, after eight days of daily inquiries came the welcome word that my lists had been approved.

"Now what do I need to do?" I asked our RA.

"You need to set up a JPay account for emails, and a Securus account for phone calls, which can only be made collect. You then need to have each of your contacts set up a JPay and Securus account on their end if they want to be able to contact you by email or phone."

He then handed me a ten-page booklet explaining how to set up both accounts.

"One last thing," he said, as I was getting up to leave his office. "You can access your email account for a half hour each day, whenever the terminal is not in use."

Upon my return to my cube, I heaved myself up on my upper bunk, and began leafing through the handbook. Reading through the JPay instructions, I saw that each email would cost forty cents for up to one page of text. I realized I'd soon go broke if I sent anywhere near the volume of emails I did on the outside. That wouldn't be happening, though. We were limited to a half hour's access per day, and to thirty approved contacts. The instructions were so damn complicated that I doubted there'd be many of my contacts willing to go through all the necessary hoops to set up an account.

Just when I thought that nothing could possibly be any worse than the email morass, I started flipping through the Securus phone account instructions. I reached the part where it stated that long-distance rates were nine cents per minute, and we could talk with each approved contact for up to an hour per week, and realized that phone calls just to Linda were going to be costing me about $22 a month, or $220 for the ten months I would be stuck here. Figuring I'd be emailing Linda alone at least once daily, that would be another thirty emails at forty cents per email for $12 a month, or $120 for the ten months of my stay. Suddenly the three grand I'd salvaged for my commissary account didn't seem like all that much. I then rolled over and buried my face in my pillow.

A few minutes later, after I'd flipped over and was lying listlessly on my upper bunk, Leo dropped by, dripping with sweat from the tennis class he'd just finished teaching.

"So did your contacts list get approved yet, Kel?" he asked while returning his tennis racket to his locker.

"Yeah, but those JPay instructions are so complicated. And those phone call rates? We'd have to work an eight-hour day at twelve cents an hour just to be able to afford a ten-minute call!"

"Yeah, the JPay email account set-ups are a pain in the ass. If you can get two or three people on the outside willing to set one up, you'll be doing well, my friend. But forget those rates Securus quoted you. Those are for long distance calls. Have your wife set up a Google Voice account, with a local Taft number that can then be forwarded to her cell phone. That way you'll only have to pay twenty-three cents per call, and the calls can be up to an hour in length."

"Wow, really? That's awesome! As soon as I get my JPay account set up, I'll email her and let her know."

So for the next ten days, I managed to exchange three emails with Linda, as it took a while to get both accounts set up and running smoothly. As soon as I managed to email Linda the Google voice instructions, she was able to get an account set up with a local Taft number, and we had a couple of hour long calls on each of her two days off.

But that had been it. Three emails and two phone calls during my first three weeks at Taft. I could easily have had that many interactions on the outside within a matter of minutes. But then again, five deep-souled interactions were at least better than none.

One of the most depressing daily rituals of all was mail call. Each day at around three in the afternoon, we'd all huddle with a mixture of anticipation and dread at the front of Dorm C while a guard with a bag full of mail began calling out the names of all the lucky recipients. It was impossible not to feel jealous of all those whose names were called, and especially of those called multiple times. And there was no emptier feeling than when the guard had finally reached the bottom of the bag. I would trudge wearily back to my cube empty-handed.

To spend time in prison was to be dehumanized. My name no longer mattered, especially since it never got called during mail call, one of the few times it could. Instead, I was now Prisoner 57145-112. I felt like I was living in the world of George Lucas' film *THX-1138*, where free will is outlawed by means of mandatory medication that controls human emotion and everyone is identified by their ID number. I forced myself to memorize my new identity.

Everyone must wear grey and white, as no colored clothing could be sold in commissary. I was living in a grey and white world. Taft's desert location magnified this sense of dust and doom, as the sand sucked the life out of the landscape and left me longing for a glimpse of green.

But perhaps there could still be a silver lining. One of my dorm-mates had told me that the most sought-after work detail was in the Native American Garden. The job was outdoors, but we were sheltered from the desert heat by the trees, there was lots of physical labor, like raking and planting and watering the trees, and it was far and away the least supervised of all the possible jobs due to its remote location. So I'd started volunteering in the Native American Garden during my first week here. I loved it. Now I'd had to change my religion to Native American to do it, but since Pops was part Native Canadian and my foster sister Diane was full First Nations, I figured why not. But volunteering was only an option for the first month, when you could not be required to work.

That first month was rapidly ending, as in another week and a half's time I was facing the dreaded prospect of becoming a slave, forced to work, like everyone else, for twelve cents an hour. I had two deeply cherished values which were about to go to war: my love of being outdoors and relatively unsupervised, versus my hatred of being a slave. Ultimately, one would have to be sacrificed at the altar of the other. But which one? Once upon a time I'd been a slave to both Mom and God, and hated it. I wouldn't do that again.

CHAPTER 6

THE BIRTH OF MARTYR KEL AND WRITER KEL

1970-1989

It was the spring of 1970. When Mom forced me get up early every Sunday, get dressed up, and go with her and Pops and my sister Shauna to the Christian and Missionary Alliance Church – which was pretty much the same as the hellfire and brimstone Baptist church down the block – I started to feel like Mom and God were the same person.

Six days a week, Mom yelled at me, whenever I dared to defy her, "Your will must be broken, young man." I must have been really bad for her to keep telling me this. On the seventh day, she handed over the reins to the church. Every Sunday morning, the Alliance pastor thundered from his pulpit, "Your will must be broken. You must die to self, in order to live for God." I'd much rather have been out playing with our miniature collie Duchess than listening to this.

By the spring of 1971, we'd already moved three times in the six years I'd been with this family. Every time we'd move, Mom would give us kids the same speech: "Look how much I've sacrificed for you." And once again, she'd hand me over to the church on Sundays. The Alliance pastor would thunder from his pulpit, "Look how much Jesus sacrificed for you. He suffered and died a horrible, painful death for your sins."

By the time the evangelist Terry Winter came to Victoria in the spring of 1971, I was terrified that I was gonna burn in hell for my horribly unbroken will. When that preacher man gave that altar call, I broke down weeping, rushed down to the front of that auditorium, and turned my life over to Jesus as a fire insurance policy. At least now, having already been abandoned by two moms, my hope was that even if my newest mom abandoned me, hopefully Jesus wouldn't. In that moment I became Martyr Kel.

None of my elementary school friends were Christians. My best friend Alan didn't believe in God. This made me embrace my role as the defender of the faith among my circle of friends that much more. It also helped keep me humble. If Alan could be such a kind human without God, why did I need God so much?

None of my junior high or high school friends were Christians either, which meant mostly that I never got invited to any of the cool parties, as being a Christian for me meant not drinking and not smoking, which is what most of the cool people were doing at those parties.

Yet God managed to use me most powerfully whenever I was forced to truly acknowledge what a mess I was. When I was on a junior high track team trip to Hawaii and was feeling suicidal because I hadn't been invited to any parties because I didn't drink, one of my teammates came back from a party and started pouring out his heart to me about how empty his life felt. Having felt empty myself that night, God was able to use my willingness to acknowledge my own emptiness to help my teammate see that God still loved us both.

When I was in college, God used me most powerfully when I was hating my major, and so looked to feed my soul by volunteering with Teen Challenge, getting to know the street kids in downtown Vancouver each Monday night. Just like my best friend Alan, whose kindness challenged me to be a better Christian, the resilience of those street kids, despite lacking all the comforts of home I took for granted, also challenged me to ask myself what difference having God meant to how I lived my life.

When I was hating the world at the spring banquet of my first year at Pepperdine Law School, as I'd blown my scholarship and knew I couldn't afford to come back the next fall, on the ride home from the afterparty a classmate poured her heart out to me about how she'd had an abortion and couldn't believe that God could still love her. I then shared with her about how amazed I'd been that Pops and God could still love me despite my having blown my scholarship, and continued to encourage her that she was loved by God for the rest of the semester. At a beach party at the end of that school year, that same classmate rushed over to me, threw her arms around my neck, and said, "You know how you've been trying to show God's love to me these past few weeks? Well, you got through!"

* * * * *

I remembered what my Mom said about her and Pops choosing to adopt my sister and me. I didn't know anyone else but us who was adopted. I decided that my sister and I must be from another culture, the "adopted" culture. I also heard Pops calling me "Special K" all the time. *Wow,* I thought to myself, *it must be special to be from another culture.* And with that letter to the editor I wrote as a seven year old about integration being a wonderful thing, as we could learn so much from other cultures, Writer Kel, my truest, deepest self, was born.

Pops always loved the little sci-fi short stories I wrote in elementary school, like the one about how if chickens ruled the world, they'd be eating at Kentucky Fried Humans. I didn't truly fall in love with writing, though, until my last year of high school, when my Careers teacher, John Clazie, and my English teacher both had us keep a journal. My English teacher had told us on the first day of class that she was an atheist, but when I wrote a lot about God in my stream of consciousness ramblings in my journal, she rewarded me for not editing myself for her sake by changing my grade from a B+ to an A. I'd finally found a place where I belonged, as Writer Kel.

After mom told me I didn't need to go to college to be a hotel manager, however, I had to bury Writer Kel and major in something safe like business rather than something I was passionate about like English and ignore the urging of my college English professor to change my major.

Once I became an immigration lawyer, the best Writer Kel could hope for was to be Lawyer Kel's fragile sidekick, which is why I kept taking writing classes every year.

Three things had kept me alive before I landed in prison: my faith in God, reading, and writing. Prison took me back to those three things, as my spiritual hunger deepened, inspiring me to go to chapel every week and join the Christian School of Ministry. And I read everything I could find in the prison library.

CHAPTER 7

RELIEF

May 2013

One of the first books I read once I got to Taft was *American Gods,* by Neil Gaiman. And that novel's opening, with the central character, Shadow, feeling a sense of relief when he landed in prison, really resonated with me. Sure, the Feds had taken aim at me and taken me down, but they had emptied their last bullet in doing so, and here I was, still breathing. So rather than having destroyed me, they'd merely shattered my false selves to the point where I was finally, hopefully ready to be remade into something a little closer to my true self.

Paul had invited me to take the recently vacated lower bunk in his cube and had mistakenly convinced his cube-mate Don in our Taft Federal Prison C Dorm that at least I would be an improvement over their last, Hispanic, cube-mate. Don, however, whose bed was the epitome of military grade neatness, assumed that I, being white like him, would similarly be obsessively tidy. Nothing could have been further from the truth.

As soon as I moved into my new cube, I filled almost all of my entire four shelves of the locker with the thirty sci-fi novels I had checked out of the prison library at that time. The rest of my section of the locker was jammed full of the regulation coffin-grey prison shorts, grey tank tops, grey t-shirts, white boxers, white socks and grey sweats I'd been forced to buy from the prison commissary, along with the cans of tuna I'd been forced to buy in order to have anything semi-healthy to eat, and the lemons and oranges I'd bought, which I would then mix with the sugar packets I'd steal from the cafeteria to make my Kel-lemonade and Kel-OJ. Inspired by all the sci-fi novels I'd been reading, I'd created a sci-fi alter ego for myself name Kel-Dar, who could cope with the absurdity of prison life way better than I could. Kel-Dar was trying to make the best of things.

Scattered all over my rumpled sheets were a half-dozen or more of the novels I was reading at any given time, binders full of notes from the Christian School of Ministry classes I was taking, and three or four legal pads I was obsessively attempting to write the middle third of my memoir on in the voice of my sci-fi alter ego Kel-Dar. There was not a lot of space left for me to sleep, but I found I slept best amidst all that clutter.

Whatever I couldn't find space for on the bed or in my portion of the locker, I would try to find boxes for. Each morning before bed inspections, I'd hurriedly shove everything I could into those boxes and then shove them under the bed. I always made sure that I was lying in bed when they did the inspections, as that way they wouldn't be able to see all the stuff I was lying on top of.

Another character I related to was Ransom of Thulcandra, from C.S. Lewis' *Out of the Silent Planet*. Like Ransom, I was a little afraid, and my journey so far had been incredibly painful but would hopefully eventually prove healing, and I'd likely be deemed crazy or courageous, or both, before its end.

I had now spent about three weeks of my ten-month sentence here in Taftghanistan, and the clarity I felt during my eight-day stay at MDC has begun to reveal itself once again.

For while the associate warden may have tried to sow whatever fear he could into us during our "admissions and orientation" session by warning us he had his "confidential informants" (aka CI's, aka rats, aka lying assholes, etc.), in our midst, the effort was wasted on me. For, as eBay – whose nickname came from his ability to score us the Reeboks that cost sixty bucks in commissary for just twenty bucks – had put it rather succinctly, there are only two types of people in federal prison: "rats" and "those who get ratted on". And by taking me into his confidence, he was telling me that he knew that I belonged to the latter group.

And my further hope was that I would continue finding new ways to transform my madness into my bravery. For while many may well have considered my decision to hang out with the Black inmates while

I was at MDC sheer madness, to me it was just the opposite. I felt that the only way I could avoid the madness of my old life spent desperately trying to please everyone else was by being brave enough to do what I needed to do for myself. Even though I'd thought at the time that I became a lawyer for myself, looking back I now realize that it was just another way for me to try to please others, and even save others, so I could feel more like I belonged.

CHAPTER 8

THE BIRTH OF LAWYER KEL

1985-1989

By the summer of 1985, just as I was beginning my two-year vacation back home in Victoria to recover from my traumatic first year at Pepperdine Law School, Sherwin-Williams of Canada, the company Pops had worked for his whole career, went bankrupt. Their American parent company, meanwhile, had created a partnership known as BAPCO with C-I-L, Inc., of Canada, in 1984. When Sherwin-Williams of Canada went bankrupt, C-I-L swooped in and got rid of all their senior managers, including Pops.

Pops the provider was forced to become Pops the survivor.

No matter how hard Pops tried to find another managerial position which would enable him to make the best use of his more than a quarter of a century with Sherwin-Williams, the only job he could find was as a traveling salesman with Glidden Paints. Victoria is the capital of British Columbia, but it is still a small town, and so the job with Glidden meant that Pops would have to move from our reasonably comfortable lower middle-class home in Victoria, on Vancouver Island, to camping out in a tent trailer in White Rock, on the lower mainland.

Eventually, Pops managed to scrape together enough money from his new job to move our small family to Aldergove. I had to stay behind in Victoria with a family from our church until I could finally arrange a transfer with my employer, B.C. Ferries, from Swartz Bay on Vancouver Island to Tsawassen on the lower mainland.

Pops was a survivor, all right, and before long our family was reunited in our new Aldergrove home. I still hadn't succeeded in saving enough money to be able to afford a return to Pepperdine Law School, though. I'd blown my shot at renewing my scholarship by failing to stay in the top ten percent during my first year there, and I couldn't get financial aid as I didn't have a green card.

One day Mom noticed a tiny ad in the paper for a green card lottery and encouraged me to apply. The year was 1986, the first year of the diversity visa lottery program, and it was wide open. You could enter as often as you liked if each entry was mailed separately. I half-heartedly applied, sending in about a dozen applications. I was too cheap to spend any more on postage than that.

When I was miraculously chosen for an interview, the consular officer asked me how many applications I'd submitted.

"About a dozen," I replied.

"That's all?" he answered. "Everybody else I've interviewed today said they'd sent hundreds."

There was still one big problem, though. I had to convince the officer that I would not become a public charge if I was issued my immigrant visa to be able to come to the United States and be granted permanent resident status. My primary motivation for entering the green card lottery, however, was so that I could become a public charge by applying for financial aid based on my new, improved immigration status.

To make matters worse, I'd foolishly invested the few savings I'd scraped together during my year and a half back in Canada in a penny stock, so I had no real savings to try to impress the officer with. Instead of savings, I proudly showed him my stock certificate. He fell for it and issued me my immigrant visa.

Thank God! A week after my successful immigrant visa interview, the CEO of the company I'd invested in absconded with most of the firm's remaining cash, and my stocks became worthless overnight. Boy, was I ever going to become a massive public charge!

After a couple of years off, which is the longest break you can take since once you start, you must finish law school within five years, I returned to Malibu in the fall of 1987. This time around was more fun than my disastrous first year at Pepperdine. With financial aid, thanks to my new green card status, I no longer needed to worry about having to try to stay in the top ten percent of my class.

During that year, I applied for Pepperdine's London program, as I'd always loved to travel, so I could go abroad for the first semester of my final year. I'd heard how expensive rent could be in London. Creativity was key. I knew that Pepperdine was a Church of Christ school, so I figured out what the equivalent church in England would be and gave that church a call. I asked if anyone in their congregation might be willing to offer affordable room and board to a starving student. Ask, and you shall receive, as the pastor provided me with the name and number of the Mardle family in Downham, Bromley, Kent.

The Mardles welcomed me into their quaint little cottage in late August of 1988 for just a hundred dollars a month for room and board.

After I learned of Pops' traumatic brain injury from a near-fatal car crash during my first few weeks there, I spent the semester in a daze. And when I flew home and saw him that Christmas, I could barely recognize the frail skeletal figure in that hospital bed. My once powerful Pops was no more.

When I returned to Malibu in January, my studies took on a whole new relevance. I took a class in immigration law taught by Lauren Mathon, who was an immigration judge. Suddenly a light began to dawn that the things I was learning in the classroom could impact peoples' lives. Hopefully, I'd be able to save a few immigrants, and myself.

CHAPTER 9

FIFTY

May 22, 2013

If anyone had suggested to me, five years earlier, that I'd be celebrating my fiftieth birthday in the middle of the California desert, I'd have been thrilled. I'd have imagined that my friends had organized the rave to end all raves for me, with Moby as the surprise DJ.

It just so happened that I did end up celebrating my fiftieth birthday in the middle of the California desert. To say that I was less than thrilled would be the understatement of the century.

I stirred groggily in my upper metal bunk at around 5:45 in the morning of May 22, 2013, about three and a half weeks into my sentence. I clambered down to the floor and stumbled blearily to the communal restroom to brush and floss my teeth. Wandering back to my cube, I threw on my commissary purchased coffin grey sweats, coffin grey t-shirt, and bird-shit white socks, the discounted black and white Reeboks eBay had helped me obtain, and the tattered white baseball cap Leo had gifted me with.

Our dorm, Alpha Four Charlie, was the first to be released from lockdown at six am that morning, and we descended the stairs from our upper-level dorm and ambled across the dusty prison yard to line up in front of the chow hall for breakfast.

As soon as I entered the chow hall, I suddenly recalled the "no baseball cap" rule, and quickly slid it off my head and down into the right front pocket of my sweats.

Too late.

Raoul, who, at five foot eight, was one little ball of hate and the most feared of all the guards, had seen me enter the hallowed halls of chow with my forbidden head gear.

"Hey, you. Drop that tray and come over here right now!" he barked.

The 'drop that tray' line was one I'd never heard before.

"Yes, sir," I replied, depositing my empty breakfast tray in the stack next to the entrance.

"Thought you could get away with wearing that baseball cap in here, did you?" he snarled.

"No sir, I for-" I began.

"Shut the fuck up. No breakfast for you. Go sit down at one of those empty tables near the exit. I'll let you know what your extra duty is when I'm good and ready."

"Yes, sir," I answered, and went and slumped down at an empty table at the far end of the chow hall. We'd all seen our fellow inmates get punished with extra duty for breaking some bullshit rule or another. I'd never heard of anyone being deprived of a meal as well. I mean sure, the food sucked, but still, there wasn't going to be a chance to eat again for at least another five hours, as lunch didn't start until 11 am.

A half hour or so later, after I'd finished reading *The New Yorker* magazine I'd found lying on one of the tables, Raoul strolled over and said, "Clean up these ten tables closest to the exit, and then get the fuck out of here."

I proceeded to clean up those ten tables in record time, as I didn't want to linger any longer than necessary over the sight of any food left behind. I did, however, make sure I pocketed all the sugar packets I could find so I could use them later to sweeten the lemonade I was going to make to celebrate my birthday, with the lemons I had bought in commissary the day before. I then headed over to the track and met up with my Irish-German friend Red, and we began our morning walk. As we ambled our usual sixteen laps around the track, for our daily four miles, I told him about what had just happened at breakfast.

"You've gotta write Raoul up for that, dude. The guards aren't allowed to deprive us of meals."

Red had been an accountant on the outside, but was one of a very small number who had actually taken his case to trial. When he ended up losing and got hit with the "trial penalty" of a greatly extended sentence for having dared to go to trial, he channeled his anger at the injustice he'd suffered into helping his fellow inmates fight for their rights. Red had quickly developed a reputation as the best jailhouse lawyer in our facility, having already won reduced sentences for several of our fellow inmates by helping them prepare their appeals.

"Yeah, something didn't seem right about that. Let me think about it."

Once we got done with our four miles, I headed back up to our dorm. I went over to Leo and asked him if he thought I should write Raoul up.

"Hell, no," Leo replied instantly. "He'll come after you for sure, man. You'll have a target on your back for the rest of your time here. Just keep your head down and stay the hell out of his way."

What the fuck was I supposed to do? On the one hand, I knew Raoul had abused his power, probably not for the first time, and needed to be held accountable. On the other hand, I didn't want to have to spend the next seven months or longer looking over my shoulder, in constant fear as to how he might retaliate.

Red dropped by my cube a few minutes later.

"So are you ready to write Raoul up?" he asked.

"I don't know, man. I'm afraid he might come after me if I do."

"You can't let him get away with that shit. It just emboldens him. Let's go see what Brad thinks, before he heads home for the day."

"All right."

Brad was our dorm's unit manager. He served as the liaison between us inmates and the prison staff.

Red and I hustled down to Brad's office, as we knew his office hours would be ending soon. Fortunately, we caught him just as he was about to leave.

"Do you have a few minutes?" Red asked him.

"Sure, come on in," Brad replied.

Red and I sat down across from him in his tiny office. I described what had happened, what Red had recommended, and why I was afraid of taking Red's advice.

"He crossed a line by depriving you of a meal. Red's right. You've gotta write this guy up."

"Ok, what do I need to do?"

Brad then slid the forms I needed to fill out across the table to me. I filled them out quickly and handed them back to him.

Later that day, eBay dropped by my cube and sang "Happy Birthday" to me. After he left, I wept quietly in my bunk. It was my favorite birthday gift ever.

Of course, the mouthwatering homemade burrito, caramelized popcorn balls, and sweet caramel and nut drenched banana eBay prepared for me later that evening came a close second.

Red encouraging me to stand up for myself in response to Raoul rounded out the top three.

Best belated birthday gift? The news I received, three days later, that Raoul had been placed on indefinite administrative leave. Spending my fiftieth birthday in the middle of the California desert, though not at all in the way I would have chosen it, still managed to have its occasional moments of sweetness.

Just as my being an immigration lawyer once had.

CHAPTER 10

LOVE BEING A LAWYER

1989-1995

Once I graduated and got done taking the July 1989 bar, I called Ira Bank, whom I'd clerked for during my last semester, and asked him if he needed anyone.

"How soon can you start?"

"How's tomorrow sound?"

"Great! I've got seven Chinese clients who were part of the Tiananmen pro-democracy demonstrations. I need you to go interview them for possible asylum claims."

When I arrived at the El Dorado Motel where they were being detained, the only thing that seemed a little off was the barbed wire running along the top of it.

The young Immigration Officer guarding the front gate asked me, in heavily accented English, "Are you a liar?" and I laughed and answered "I hope not. I'm a law clerk. The lawyer I work for sent me out here today to interview these clients of his." I showed him a list which made up a group we had nicknamed the "China 7." I signed in, leaving my driver's license with him, and he led me down the hall to the makeshift hotel cell they had been piled into. There were four rusty bunkbeds nearly filling the room, and we did our best to carve out a small space in which to talk. Lu was the lone member of the group who spoke English, and so volunteered to translate for me. "The seven of us were peacefully protesting for democracy in Tiananmen Square earlier this summer," he began. "When the government troops rolled in with tanks and began beating and killing many of our friends, we fled the square." He had jagged scars on his face and arms.

"How did you get those scars?" I inquired.

"I was found shortly after the demonstrations. They detained me for ten days, and tortured me for most of that time, but I refused to reveal the names of any of the organizers. My family begged them to release me, and they finally did after my family paid a bond of about a month's salary. I then went into hiding. After a few months I managed to stow away on a ship and come to America."

It was his eyes that haunted me most. They spoke of a pain and hope too deep for words. "I will fight for you," I said, and grasped his outstretched hand. They needed me, and that was all I needed to know.

When I first saw Joseph, he was wearing black Dockers and a white dress shirt and exuded an air of confidence that I found intoxicating. He was a Hong Kong-born immigrant working in Swanson and Swanson's immigration law office, whose round face was brought into sharp focus by his watchful eyes.

"I'm Joseph. You are?" he began, fastening his gaze on me as he entered the break room after me.

"Kelly, the new associate."

"This is my senior paralegal, Joseph," Otto intervened. "If you have any questions about labor certifications, which are employment-based applications for permanent residence, Joseph's your man," he said, grasping Joseph firmly by the shoulder. I was finding it hard to breathe with all the testosterone in the room.

"Not for long," Joseph whispered to me as Otto briskly departed. "I'm putting in my two weeks' notice tomorrow. I'm going to go set up my own consulting office. How about you? Planning on staying long?"

"Hoping to, yeah. Steve seems like a great guy. Still trying to figure out Otto, though," I said as I tried to find space for my homemade lunch in the rather full fridge.

"You should think about working for yourself, too, man."

"Not my thing. Love being a lawyer, hate running an office."

"Suit yourself, Kel."

True to his word, Joseph would then spend the next nine years building his consulting business into an extremely lucrative operation. I, by contrast, would end up breaking the associate attorney longevity record by sticking around for six years. Unlike Joseph, back then I much preferred the safety of being a junior associate to the risks of trying to set up and run my own office.

About a year after I joined Swanson and Swanson, in the fall of 1991, a Chinese calligrapher client of mine dropped by the office. "Thanks so much for all those hours you spent fighting for me to help me get my green card," he began, grasping my hand warmly. "Here's a small token of my appreciation," he said as he slowly unfurled a beautiful calligraphy scroll he had created for me. The inscription was in traditional Chinese characters, which he translated for me as meaning, "You will help many people, and/or make history, with the power of your words. And your words will have the power to express the taste of knives."

God, how I loved being an immigration lawyer. All those years of study, that near nervous breakdown in my first semester at Pepperdine Law School, all that was washed away in the bliss of being able to try to save my client's lives.

Haunted by the scars of Lu Wei, my very first client, who had been tortured by the Chinese authorities for refusing to give up the names of his fellow demonstrators at Tiananmen Square, I promised him I would fight for him. And when I finally won his case, his tears as he grasped my hand in court that day would swim in my soul for the next two decades plus.

When I wept and prayed, a few years later, with my Nigerian client Abike as she tearfully told me of her bleeding ulcers from the stress of her incarceration at the Terminal Island Detention Center, I promised her I would fight for her release. So when her husband Barine called and left me the message that he'd managed to borrow enough money from friends to bond her out, I sat alone in my hotel room in San Francisco and wept silent tears of joy. When all I had initially been able to do for Abike was to weep and pray with her, I had begun to see that there were often limits to what I could for my clients as a lawyer. From that day forward, my soul was split in two between my lawyer self and my writer self, as I'd been taking writing classes ever since I'd become a lawyer. I promised myself that whenever I found myself unable to help my immigrant clients as a lawyer, that I would do whatever I could to someday give voice to their cries for justice as a writer.

For Lu Wei, for Abike, and for many, if not most, of my immigrant clients over the course of my twenty-three-year career as an immigration lawyer, one of the hardest things for them to do was to trust. Nothing was secure, nothing was stable, and living as they now were in an adopted country, they too had begun to lose any real sense of what home really felt like. As an adopted child who spent the first eleven months of my life in a foster home, I knew how they felt.

Together, Lu Wei, Abike, and my other immigrant clients and I slowly managed to form bonds cemented by our separate yet somehow similar primal wounds. It wasn't easy, but we managed to slowly learn to trust each other as we came to see that we shared a common enemy: a heartless bureaucracy. This enemy had many faces, from the naked cruelty of the mainland Chinese torturers of Lu Wei, to the cold indifference of the Terminal Island jailers who were deaf to the pleas of their own prison doctors begging them to release Abike.

Together, we found ways to help each other feel a little more like we belonged, in a world which usually left us feeling like outsiders. Lu Wei's asylum approval and Abike's release on bond helped to remind them that there were still people in the world willing to acknowledge their suffering and to offer them some relief from it.

Lu Wei's tearful cradling of my hands, and Abike's husband Barine's joyous message on my San Francisco hotel room phone informing me his wife had been released, helped to remind me that I truly was living out the calling I'd adopted from Simone Weil for my undergrad senior yearbook quote, to be *able to give someone in affliction exactly the help required to save him, at the supreme moment of his need.* Being an immigration lawyer was a place where I could feel that I truly belonged.

Being in prison, however? Not so much.

CHAPTER 11

HEALTHCARE DELAYED IS HEALTHCARE DENIED

May-June 2013

After I injured my Achilles tendon on Memorial Day weekend, it was almost two weeks before I finally got to see a camp doctor. At least Doctor R had a sense of humor. After examining my Achilles, he announced that I should have no problem returning to the job I'd been volunteering at during my first month in the Native American Garden.

"Just dig with your other leg," he helpfully suggested.

When I replied that there might be some liability issues for the prison if I aggravate my injury, he rather reluctantly wrote me a note authorizing me to be off work for a couple more weeks, and gave me an Ace bandage and some pain meds.

A week later, I met with Doctor H, who was Doctor R's twin, minus the sense of humor. I told Doctor H about how much pain I was still in and showed him how bruised and swollen my Achilles still was.

"So I guess I'll be needing an MRI, right?" I asked.

"No, no MRI is indicated for that type of injury."

Which is strange, because when another inmate, with an injury identical to mine, came back from seeing Doctor H later that same day, he told me that the doctor had recommended an MRI for him. Oh well, I thought to myself, at least we get to see doctors here. At some prison camps, they have none.

I'd been unable to work in the Native American Garden, or work out, since injuring my Achilles a week earlier, and was afraid to do either for at least another week or so, for fear of re-injuring it. And now I'd developed further symptoms: bruising around my right ankle, which could indicate either that my Achilles was torn, or that blood vessels burst in the area of my injury, and swelling of my left foot, which had forced me to start sleeping with both feet elevated and to spend considerable time each day – like now, for example – with both feet elevated above the level of my heart, not exactly a prime position to be trying to write from.

My fears were multiple. I feared re-injuring my Achilles, I feared being permanently hobbled by my injury, I feared losing my job over at the Native American Garden, which was supposed to officially start this coming week, as I had been simply volunteering before, if I were sidelined by this injury for much longer, and I feared gaining even more weight if I was unable to work or work out for much longer. I had already gained between five and ten pounds since my arrival a month earlier, despite how active I had tried to be for the first three weeks or so prior to my injury, as they fed us for twenty-five cents a day, mostly rice and beans.

I feared a growing sense of disconnection with the outside world. While I'd been slowly acclimating to my new environment in the month or so I'd been here in Taftghanistan, one of the toughest aspects of being here had been a growing sense of isolation from the outside world, coupled with a deep desire to not be a burden to the tiny handful of angels on the outside with whom I have managed to maintain my tenuous connection to that world.

My regular routine had degenerated to little more than eating, sleeping (with no working or working out allowed until my Achilles healed), reading, writing, taking School of Ministry classes two nights a week and going to chapel one night a week, while by contrast my handful of connections on the outside were leading insanely busy lives, what with work, school, and/or family commitments leaving them exhausted just trying to make it through each day.

While my life had gotten dramatically un-busy, my handful of outside connections' lives had gotten exponentially busier. Couple that with phone and email service which seemed deliberately designed to confuse those on the outside, and it was a recipe for increasing one's sense of isolation to an extraordinary degree.

Another fear was that whatever survival skills I might be developing to adapt to my new institutional environment would likely have little or no relevance to whatever survival skills I might need to re-orient myself back to life on the outside upon my release.

In addition to the literal prison I now found myself in, I had to find a way to break free of the much deeper bondage of being a "prisoner in the house of fear" (also known as "LawLand").

The first step to breaking free of this bondage would be to acknowledge its hold on me, and to acknowledge its intergenerational origins, both from my maternal adoptive grandfather (whose best friend was killed by the IRA, and who buried his feelings in the bottle) and adoptive mom (who buried her feelings from being the only child of an abusive alcoholic father), as well as from my birthfather (who buried his feelings from being the son of a tough-love father), all three of whom were similarly unknowingly "prisoners in the house of fear", as all three were similarly burdened with the "curse of buried feelings". The second step to breaking free of this bondage would be to turn to God and echo the cry of the psalmist in Psalm 79:8a, "Do not hold against us the sins of past generations..."

I turned once again to the Bible for help, and I found it. The answer to escaping this prison of fear seemed to lie in those enigmatic words of brother Jesus, when he gave us the following call in Matthew 10:16: "I am sending you out as sheep among wolves, therefore be wise as serpents, and as gentle as doves." I had all too often erred in striving only to be as "gentle as doves" without the necessary "wisdom of the serpent", and so the "getting of wisdom" had proven to be exceedingly painful.

Solomon wisely reminded us in Proverbs 4:7, "The beginning of wisdom is this: wisdom is supreme, therefore get wisdom. Though it cost you all you have, get understanding." And as he went on to remind us in Proverbs 4:22, "Above all else, guard your heart, for everything you do flows from it." And "getting understanding" certainly had "cost me all I had".

My heart's desire was therefore twofold, now that I had "lost almost all I had": that I might slowly begin to get understanding as to how I had managed to lose it all, and how I could avoid suffering similar catastrophic losses in the future, and hopefully help others avoid them as well; and further, that I might "guard my heart" from its at times almost overwhelming fear of abandonment, which had caused it to blindly ignore the dangers of being driven by those fears to the brink of destruction.

My hope and prayer was that both my life and art might manage to return to the place where my head and my heart could finally merge, and find their true home at last.

"Greatest scam," sneered one of my dormmates as he watched me hobble up the two flights I needed to navigate six times a day for chow, with my Ace-bandaged right leg and cane for support.

"You mean this prison?" I replied.

"No, your knee. Lots of us wish we could pull a scam like that so we could get a lower bunk."

"But I don't want a lower bunk."

"Then what do you want?"

"An MRI for the Achilles injury I suffered almost a month ago, as the pain, the bruising, and the swelling have all been getting worse, not better."

"That'll never happen."

Of course, everything about federal prison is a scam.

So anything we inmates can try to pull to try to level the playing field is completely justified, as far as I'm concerned.

So yes, of course I was going to milk my Achilles injury for all it was worth. I mean, if hyping my injury meant that they could not force me to work for twelve cents an hour, why wouldn't I? And if not being forced to work meant that I could hang out in the dugout next to the baseball field all day? And if hanging out in the dugout all day meant that I could read a book every four days, and write the rest of the time? I can't imagine why anybody in their right mind would not want to pull off something like that.

So despite what I'd just told my fellow inmate, yes, it was a scam, one of my favorites of my time there. Unlike Joseph's scam which had landed me in prison, this was a scam I could benefit from.

During the first six weeks or so I spent at Taft Federal Prison, I became good friends with an African American graphic designer named Holiday, whose favorite place had been in the dugout next to the baseball field. We bonded immediately over our artistic passions, and I knew I was gonna miss our conversations once he left. The day before his release, as the two of us were hanging out there, he said to me, "This place is yours now. Take good care of it."

It would turn out to be one the best gifts anyone ever gave me during my ten months in federal prison.

As soon as Holiday was released, I hastily staked my claim to the dugout he'd bequeathed me, and lugged my bag of books, legal pads and pens out there and set up shop. The first day after his departure, there were a couple of guys already there, sharing stock tips, but after a few minutes of peaceful co-existence, they eventually moved on. Each day after lunch, I'd head out there to read and write before anybody else could get any ideas about trying to take over my space. Since the multi-racial gang I'd decided to create in order to ease tensions during my time in prison was called the "Principled Rebels", the dugout soon became known as the "Principled Rebels' Clubhouse." And once I began writing outdoors, I couldn't believe how dramatically the quality of my writing improved. I saw how chaotic and obsessively internalized my writing had been while I was cooped up in my little piece of purgatory known as the dorm, and how my writing had begun to grow wings once I was able to put pen to paper in my little piece of paradise behind home plate.

Hanging out in my Principled Rebels Clubhouse in the dugout behind the baseball diamond at Taft Federal Prison, drinking my Kel-lemonade I'd made with commissary-bought lemons and sugar packets I'd stolen from the prison cafeteria, I imagined myself back in my childhood dream home, my treehouse, and felt safe at last. My treehouse in the forest behind my childhood home, which I'd built out of scrap lumber from a nearby construction site, had been my heaven. Back in April of 1995, however, I'd spent some time in hell.

CHAPTER 12

HOMICIDAL RAGE/LIFE IN LAWLAND

1995-1999

It is Monday, April 24, 1995. Just five days earlier, the Oklahoma City Federal Building has been bombed. I, however, have been off work for the past week with chronic fatigue syndrome, and so have not yet heard the news.

As my lunch bag rolls through the X-ray machine at the front entrance of the Los Angeles Federal Building, the security guard jokes, "I bet you've got a bomb in there!"

Thinking to myself that it had been a rather odd comment, and still a little hazy from my recent bout with chronic fatigue, I get on the elevator with a middle-aged white guy I've never seen before. I greet him with the words, "The security guard just joked that I probably had a bomb in my lunch."

The lone stranger seems as puzzled by the joke as I had been and exits on the third floor. I continue my climb to the eighth floor, where I exit the elevator and go meet my immigrant clients in Room 8024, and then began preparing them for their upcoming green card interview.

A few minutes later I found myself surrounded by a half dozen heavily armed cops who proceed to separate me from my lunch bag, haul me out into the hallway, cuff me hard, and shove me over to the same elevator I had just ascended in. This time I descend all the way down to the sub-basement, where I soon discover they have a holding cell. They photograph me, and then lock me in the cell.

"What's all this about?" I plead.

"Making a terrorist threat in a federal building," snarls Jose, a short, stocky Hispanic officer.

"But I was simply repeating a joke the security guard had just made," I reply.

"We take all threats seriously," Jose snaps.

Still foggy from the chronic fatigue, my fog is now rippled with terror that I've just had a sick joke played on me by the security guard. I keep calling out every name I can think of, all the different immigration officers and supervisors who both know and respect me, as I have been coming down to the federal building at least once a week for the past five and a half years.

Cop Number Two, Dion, a tall, distinguished looking Black officer, offers me a cup of water after I've been there for what feels like hours.

"Thanks!" I say.

"Don't mention it," he replies.

I then overhear Jose talking soothingly to his girlfriend on the phone. "Don't worry, dear, I'll be home soon."

Then he shifts his attention back to me, and growls, "You're going to be spending the night in jail, man, and boy do they *love* lawyers in there."

And somewhere inside me, the fragile little boy I've always been just shatters and lies crumpled on the floor of that cell.

I am finally released several hours later, with a forty-dollar citation for disturbing the peace. My criminal lawyer friend Gerald Klausner will later advise me that they were required to cite me for something to protect themselves from being sued for false imprisonment. The security guard, meanwhile, whose joke had inspired the entire affair, will never even be questioned about the incident.

I overhear Steve Swanson, the junior partner, telling his dad the next day, "He's the best associate we've ever had. This was all a misunderstanding." Otto Swanson, who was a former Border Patrol officer, replies, "He's crazy."

But that is the least of my concerns. I just need some down time, a little time off from work, to try to get my head together from what I've just been through. I wander down to the swing sets at the Culver City Veterans Center Park at the end of the block from our condo. I had spent the first eleven months of my life in the care of foster mom Grace, swinging on swing sets at the park at the end of the block, swinging on her backyard swing set, and swinging on a baby swing inside her lovely little home. Swing sets have been my safe place ever since.

I talk with an older Jewish neighbor about what I'd been through, and he encourages me to write about it. He also hands me his business card, which simply says "Storyteller," and I say, "That's what I want to be when I grow up."

I take his advice to heart, and just write. As a lawyer, much of my earlier writing had been very heady, with too little heart. This writing was much rawer. It is during this time that one of my female classmates, Pine-Niece Joshua, tells me one of the coolest things anyone has ever said about my writing. "Your head and your heart have finally merged," she says.

As I'm writing about the emotional tsunami Jose had unleashed within me during my detainment, I scare the shit out of myself by writing about my rage to want to kill that fucker. This is the first time in my life that anyone has so brutalized me that I've been forced to face the fact that I am capable of this homicidal rage. But he had so fucked with my head, for reasons I couldn't possibly begin to understand. It was utterly absurd.

Later that day, I return to the swing set in Veteran's Park. As I swing slowly up and down, I am overwhelmed by a sense of powerlessness that I do not want to analyze now. I am more afraid than I have ever been in my life, and sense vaguely that it is things in myself I fear most. I take a deep breath and try to let the swing set do its soothing work.

Instead of killing that cop, however, I take my criminal lawyer friend's advice. I pay the forty dollar fine and designate that the funds be donated to a crime victims' fund.

After my arrest at the Federal Building in 1995, however, my writing took on a new urgency, just as it had during my first semester of law school. Once again, I had suffered a major trauma. Once again, I was writing to save my life.

During that time, I was taking poetry and memoir classes at Santa Monica College. One of my classmates was Pine-Niece Joshua, who was a feature film story editor at Warner Brothers Studios. I was preparing to attend an Image Writers Conference in Taos, New Mexico, at which conference I was planning on submitting the first five pages of my memoir to multiple literary agents. Pine-Niece offered to edit my pages for me and managed to trim my rambling narrative into some really tight scenes.

Before I pitched to those agents, however, the conference organizers encouraged us all to take the Myers-Briggs Personality Test. Rick, a writer friend I'd met at an earlier conference, was administering the test, and came up to me right before I took it.

"Hi, Kel. Didn't you tell me at the last conference that you were an immigration lawyer?"

"Yeah, that's right."

"Well, then, you will most likely be ESTJ, as that's what most lawyers are."

Half an hour later, I discovered that I was INFP. The anti-lawyer. Apparently, I should have been a writer or a social worker. Oh well, I suppose immigration law is probably the closest area of law to social work, I figured.

The next day, I pitched the first five pages of my manuscript to about a dozen literary agents. The eleven who represented memoir all said basically the same thing, that I was too young and nobody knew who I was.

The one exception was Michael Pruss, who worked for Focus Features.

"Have you thought about turning this into a screenplay?"

"No, why?"

"The parallels between immigrants and adoptees would make for a great screenplay theme!"

"Wow, okay. Maybe I'll take some classes."

About ten months after my arrest, detention, and release from the holding cell in the sub-basement of the Federal Building in the spring of 1995, Otto Swanson stormed into my office one foggy February morning and said, "You're fired! Pack up your shit and get the hell out of here." I slowly rolled up the beautiful calligraphy scroll a client had designed for me and began packing six years' worth of personal belongings into a tattered cardboard box.

I staggered out the door a couple of hours later and wandered over to the park across the street from the office on Mindanao Way in Marina Del Rey. I lowered myself down onto a park bench with my battered box of belongings in my lap and wept quietly until the time I would usually have gone home.

When I arrived at the front door of our Culver City condo, my lovely Japanese American wife Linda, without my even telling her what had happened, simply threw her arms around me and exclaimed, "You're free!" And just in case I needed further evidence that I was truly free, when Otto tried to challenge my unemployment insurance claim by pretending he'd fired me for cause, I took him on and won that fight.

Linda and I had met back in the fall of 1990, two years after Pops had suffered his Traumatic Brain Injury, and a year after I'd received a letter from my birthmother Adele during the same week I passed the California Bar. After Pops had suffered his TBI, I'd feared that no one could ever possibly love me as unconditionally as he had, until both my birthmother Adele and then Linda came along and proved me wrong. We'd gotten married on August 29, 1992, and Joseph and his wife May had attended our wedding. With both Adele and Linda, I always felt like I belonged, unlike how I felt so often around the series of senior partners I would work for during my time as a lawyer. We'd wanted to have kids, but Linda had suffered a slip and fall accident at work and developed both fibromyalgia and later multiple chemical sensitivity as a result, and so our focus had shifted to restoring her health after that.

I then set up my own immigration filing service, calling it "KG's Filing Service," and proceeded to camp out on the steps of the Los Angeles Federal Building at all hours of the night, to file cases for other lawyers for the next five months or so. Before my legal skills really began to atrophy, however, I answered an ad for an associate immigration attorney with Michael Gurfinkel's office in Glendale.

"Are you willing to do all of the grunt work around here and get none of the credit for it?" asked Deborah, the warm, wise-cracking associate attorney who interviewed me.

"Absolutely," I replied. "As long as I can also get blamed whenever anything goes wrong."

"You got it!" she said. "You can start tomorrow."

Working with Deborah was great, but unfortunately the senior partner's cold, no-nonsense, all-about-appearances Filipino wife Millie ran the firm with an iron fist. The one thing I was most troubled by were what I believed to be the excessive fees the firm was charging.

Whenever I would voice those concerns, Millie would immediately respond, "We are the Rolls Royce of immigration law firms, and so our fees must reflect that." Yet since so many of our clients could barely afford Toyota Corolla rates, I would often surreptitiously slip our Corolla clients' files into my briefcase when I would go down to Immigration to inquire on the status of our Rolls Royce clients' cases, as I knew I could always inquire on three cases at one time.

Once I'd been there about a year and a half, however, Deborah had finally had enough of her battles with Millie and went off to set up her own firm. After a few months of being directly under Millie's thumb, I quickly grew desperate for a way out as well.

This time around, I answered an ad for a lawyer to handle the immigration cases for a business lawyer in Pasadena. Ron Summers, the white, middle-aged lawyer who'd placed the ad, grasped my hand warmly as I slipped into a seat across from him in the cafe of the Pasadena Hilton.

"My office is in the lobby," he began. "For some reason, my Chinese clients seem to like that. Have you ever worked in a hotel lobby before?"

"No, but in high school I learned in my Careers class that I'd make a great hotel manager."

"Perfect. How'd you like a job as a Hotel Lobby Immigration Department Manager?"

"Great! How soon can I start?"

One day during my first week there, Ron introduced me to his Chinese associate Danny, who referred most of his Chinese clients in need of immigration assistance to Ron.

"Ever heard of Nauru?" the sharply-dressed Danny asked me one afternoon.

"Nope. Should I have?" I replied.

"All you need to know about it," he continued, "is that it's a tiny little country in need of foreign investment, and that we have lots of Chinese clients looking for countries like Nauru to invest in, as by doing so they can become Nauru citizens and travel far more freely."

"And that's legal?" I inquired, tugging nervously at my wrinkled suit.

"Of course," he reassured me.

In the first decade or so of my career, the lines had been clear. I'd loved working with Steve, Deborah and Ron, and feared Otto, Millie and Danny. With Joseph, my seeming safe harbor, the lines would get muddy.

CHAPTER 13

INMATES VS CHILDREN OF GOD

June 2013

Oh my God. Did I hear that right? Did I just hear the chaplain say, with a perfectly straight face, that how he treated you was entirely up to you? That he could treat you like a child of God, or he could treat you like an inmate? Wait, didn't that same logic serve us so very well over in Abu Ghraib, where we stripped the "inmates" naked, piled them up in human pyramids, and walked them around with dog collars?

Later that day, I came to learn just how low the bar was to find oneself being treated like an 'inmate' by the chaplain. One of my dormmates, a guy named Brian, was telling me about how he'd taken the Christian School of Ministry's "Biblical Counseling" class over a year ago, but the chaplain had never gotten around to giving him a grade yet. Since Brian was about to be released, and needed to know his grade so that he could see what credits he might be able to use after his release, he'd been asking the chaplain to issue him a grade for some time now. When he got upset with the chaplain for how long he'd been stalling, and raised his voice in addressing him about it the other day, the chaplain decided that Brian was no longer entitled to "child of God" status, but instead needed to spend some time in the "SHU", or "Special Housing Unit", aka solitary confinement. Oh well, things could be worse. At least there were no human pyramids or dog collars involved.

At first I couldn't understand why the chaplain's words and actions as to whether he would treat us like an inmate or like a child of God were so triggering. Then suddenly it hit me. My adoptive mom had made me feel, for most of my life, that the only way that I could be good enough for her to treat me like a child of God was if I behaved like an inmate.

Inmates are expected to just follow orders, to just do what they're told, to not question things. As long as I got good grades, made my bed neatly enough to pass inspection, got up in time and dressed up for church, and didn't roll around in the backyard with our miniature collie Duchess and then track dirt on the carpets, Mom would love me. Acting like an inmate seemed to be the only way to ensure that Mom would treat me like a child of God.

If, by contrast, I ever dared to defy Mom, to question Mom, to disobey Mom, or, God forbid, to track dirt on Mom's precious carpets, Mom would invariably scream at me, "Your will must be broken, young man." In other words, whenever I would dare to act with the freedom of a child of God, Mom would treat me like an inmate.

A child of God is free to make mistakes, is free to question things, is free to break rules, as they are secure in their status as children of God. An inmate, by contrast, is never secure. They are not allowed to break the rules – which can be changed at a moment's notice – they are not allowed to make mistakes, they are not allowed to question the absolute authority of the rule-makers, or they will be banished to solitary or punished even more harshly.

The most bizarre element of this whole mind-fuck was that both the chaplain and my mom got the categories backwards. In their upside-down world, it was the rule-following, unquestioning inmates who ended up being rewarded by being treated like children of God.

By contrast, it was those of us principled rebels who broke the rules, who made mistakes, and who dared to question the absolute authority of the rule-makers who were then treated like inmates and punished for daring to act with the freedom of children of God and for refusing to act with the unfreedom of inmates.

My personality type suggested I would have enjoyed being a counselor. Even as a lawyer, "counselor" was the only title I'd ever really felt comfortable with. So it was no surprise that one of my favorite classes in Taft's Christian School of Ministry was the Biblical Counseling Class.

One of our homework assignments was to do mock intake interviews with our fellow inmates. My first, with an Asian dormmate named Jack, had been a lot of fun, and so I wanted to take on the guy in my dorm I felt most intimidated by, a white guy named Neil.

Unlike Jack, who agreed to be interviewed for free, Neil expected me to pay him for the privilege of interviewing him.

"How much?" I asked.

"Two cans of tuna and two popcorns," he replied.

Neil sure knew how to drive a hard bargain. Those four items were going to cost me three dollars in commissary. According to Prison Economy 101, coming up with that three dollars would mean my having to spend twenty-five hours replanting cacti and trees in one-hundred-degree heat in the Native American Garden for twelve cents an hour. As a lawyer, my hourly rate, based on what most lawyers make, would ordinarily have been at least two hundred dollars (except, of course, I'd never made anything close to that while working with Joseph). Neil was expecting me to pay him the equivalent of five thousand dollars in non-prison earnings for a half hour long interview.

"Sure, no problem," I answered.

Once I'd finished asking him all the psychological questions a therapist might ask a first-time patient, I had one follow-up question for him. "So, do you think I'd make a good therapist?"

"Hell, no," he replied. "You're way too introspective. You were able to mirror me just fine, but if you want to be a truly helpful therapist, you need to be a better ladder, and assume you have some wisdom to offer me." In other words, he feared my patients might stay stuck, because I might not be able to offer them ways to lift themselves out of whatever trauma they felt trapped in.

"Yeah, well, that's probably because I was way too intimidated by your PhD in Psychology. But okay, here's one for you. When I asked you about your girlfriend, you said that she was a spiritualist, right?"

"Yes."

"And then you said that you were a materialist, and that your worldview was much more evolved than your girlfriend's, right?"

"Yes."

"Well, your girlfriend's worldview is way more evolved than yours, my friend. Your worldview will fall apart if you ever go through a trauma that defies rational explanation. Your girlfriend will make it through such a crisis, though, as she's got spiritual resources your worldview won't even allow for the existence of."

For once, I managed to find him at a loss for words.

Someone else I'd found rather intimidating, and who had likewise rarely ever been at a loss for words, had been Joseph.

CHAPTER 14

LIFE IN JOSEPH WORLD

1999-2007

In 1999, after a decade of feeling like I was desperately needed by my immigrant clients, I now felt useless working for Ron. As I listlessly played another round of solitaire, the office phone suddenly buzzed to life.

"What are you doing?" Joseph asked.

"Playing solitaire, man. Things are dead around here."

"Come on over to my office. I'd like to show you something."

"Be right over." For the rest of my life, I would mark this moment.

What else did I have going on right then? I figured I had nothing to lose if I just swung by his office.

Longing to recapture my old passion, I drove over from the Pasadena mausoleum to go see Joseph's ground floor immigration consulting office in Walnut. As soon as I walked through the front door, I was struck by the beehive of activity Joseph was presiding over.

I watched as Joseph motored around the office, answering a question from one young Chinese paralegal, flipping through a file and handing it off to another paralegal. He reminded me of my junior high best friend Tony, who was so high-energy he once nicknamed another of my best friends "tag-along" for his refusal to try to keep up with Tony's frenetic pace as he raced around a Sears store in our hometown of Victoria.

"You should come work with me," Joseph said. "I've got more work than I can handle. Many of my clients have been asking if a lawyer could go with them to their interviews or court hearings. I've always had to contract that work out. You could come onboard and be 'of counsel.' My clients would love to know who the lawyer's going to be for their whole immigration journey."

"How many clients?"

"Fifteen hundred. I've been working sixty to eighty hours a week since I left Swanson and Swanson almost ten years ago, and it's starting to pay off."

I knew Joseph had always been very involved with his church, so I asked, "Do you have any religious worker cases?"

"A few, but I'm hoping to take on more. I've been getting to know a lot of pastors at church conferences, as I'm an elder in our church. We can help a lot of immigrants, Kel, and make some good money doing it. We'd make a great team. I'd like you to come join our little family."

"Well, it's not like they've had much work for me at Ron's office lately, and I could use the money. We'll do something together."

"How's five grand a month sound?"

"Five grand a month would be wonderful."

"Great, I'll get hold of you tomorrow, Kel. My clients are going to be thrilled!"

Now, before he started letting his clients know I was coming onboard, maybe I should consider my options. And then get down to business. Like, I'm a great lawyer. A boss lawyer. And yet look at me. Fucking around with this punk consultant, and not thinking about my real business. Look at me! Shoes practically worn through. Dirty pants torn at the bottom. Dog-tired and hungry. Only one suit to my name, falling apart at the seams. Shoot, I should have had my own office by now. Why hadn't I set up over there on the Miracle Mile, like so many of my friends had? Maybe team up with another lawyer, like I did with Ron. It was a great run while it lasted. By this time I could have been making a hundred grand a year, easy.

And then I thought about the work involved in running an office. Keeping track of all those revenue and expense numbers. Making sure I make enough each month so that everyone could get paid. No wonder Ron had his Chinese rainmaker Danny, to keep those revenues rolling in. Without a rainmaker like Danny or Joseph to bring in clients, the risks of going under were too great. It made me tired to think of the work and the risk.

Running an office was essentially a dangerous game. But for whom? For Joseph, if it was his office. For me, if it was mine. I didn't mind being the number two guy, if it meant Joseph doing the bulk of the grunt work and taking most of the risks. So yeah, better to join Joseph's little family than to try starting one of my own. And I'd known Joseph for years, and he seemed easy to get along with. At first.

By the time I finished wrapping things up with Ron's office and joined Joseph a few weeks later, he had moved to a tiny space on the sixth floor of the Coast Savings Bank building in West Covina. The smaller space accentuated the volume of cases, as cabinets bursting with file folders filled almost all the available space. Joseph and I worked shoulder to shoulder in that cramped space for about a year, until he managed to negotiate a favorable lease on a large corner office with a view on the fourth floor of the building.

I would finally be free to be the passionate, idealistic immigration lawyer I'd always longed to be, while Joseph would take care of the business side of things.

I had visions of Joseph and I helping religious workers obtain temporary and eventually permanent legal immigration status as they labored to fulfill God's calling for their lives. I imagined us saving countless asylum applicants, rescuing them from being sent back to torture or death in their home countries.

How wrong I was.

For the rest of my life I would wonder if I could have made another play, played my own hand, or drawn different cards. Or was the hand played around me? Does somebody stack that fuckin' deck? It was something I never decided.

All I knew then was that after a decade of feeling like a foster kid working with a series of foster lawyers and foster firms, Joseph's consulting office seemed to offer the promise of the new adoptive home I'd been dreaming of.

A decade later, I'd be jolted awake from this dream into the nightmare he'd dragged us both into, shackles and all.

CHAPTER 15

SHACKLED

July 2013

It had been about six weeks since my injury when, one night after I'd pulled an all-nighter writing, a female guard strolled over to where I was sitting by the Ping-Pong table in the TV room around midnight and told me she'd be coming by to get me at around 3 am for my 6 am appointment with an orthopedic doctor in Bakersfield. It seems these appointments were always scheduled for 6 am, as you can't have a bunch of scary felons out terrorizing the community during normal business hours.

And so, when she returned at 3 am, I was dressed and ready to begin my second straight all-nighter. Three of my five fellow inmates, who were awakened at the same time as I, were awakened for the best of all reasons: they were either going home or being released to a halfway house. I had asked to go to a halfway house and had recently been approved to go to one in South Central on December 23rd, two months before the end of my sentence.

The remaining three of us were not nearly so lucky. Because we were being accompanied by a child of God from the low security facility next door, all four of us had to wear orange jumpsuits and be shackled, as the rules for transporting inmates mandated that the security measures for the highest security detainees must be applied to all detainees.

The guy from the other facility had a cast on his hand. One of the guys from our side had a cast on his broken left foot. The other guy from our side had a prosthetic right foot. I had my cane. All in all, I'd say we were a dangerous bunch, and highly likely to make a run for it, so it's a good thing they had us all shackled. The only advantage to my cane was that at least my hands, unlike my feet, were not cuffed together, or I would not have been able to maneuver the cane.

We shuffled into the rickety old van and were driven in darkness the forty or so miles to Bakersfield. We arrived before sunrise and stumbled off the van and into a back entrance to the orthopedic doctor's office. After about a twenty-minute wait, the doctor called me in for my examination. When he asked me to roll over from my back to my stomach, while still cuffed and shackled, I felt like a beached whale. And after all that fun, the female specialist in charge of MRIs was on vacation that day. So yet another shackled trip to Bakersfield loomed likely in my future, if I were ever going to get the MRI I had now been told I needed by three different doctors.

I watched as Officer Nimrod, the guard who would have been my boss by now had it not been for my injury, slipped through the back door of the medical office, where we all knew he was having an affair with one of the nurses. What we didn't know was that he was also leaning on them to make the lay-in notices for those of us he suspected of faking our injuries as short as possible, so that we might eventually be forced to join his workforce.

Lay-in notices were what those of us who got injured were issued, which prevented us both from being forced to work for twelve cents an hour and from working out. The latter restriction sucked, but it was a small price to pay for the former benefit. Memorial Day weekend, when I'd gotten injured, had been a banner weekend for injuries, and I'd asked each of the others who'd suffered similar injuries how long their lay-in notices had been, and they'd all been given a month.

Once I finally made it in for my appointment, the nurse handed me some more Ace bandages, and told me that, for the second straight week, my lay-in notice would just be for a week.

"Do you really think I'm gonna get my MRI in a week? As both your doctors said that I need one before I can be cleared for work duty."

"Don't ask me. I was told you get a one-week lay-in notice. You'd better be back here in a week, or you'll be on the list for work duty."

"Yeah, sure, great."

A week later, the same routine. In through the backdoor slipped Officer Nimrod. Out through the front door I went with my week-long lay-in notice.

Same for week four. And weeks five, six, seven, and eight.

Finally, on week nine, the tall brunette nurse Janine was on duty when I showed up to request an extension to my lay-in notice. When I'd self-surrendered at the facility three months earlier, she'd been the first person to treat me like a human being. I hoped against hope her humanity hadn't faded in this soul-killing place.

Unlike the nurses who'd robotically issued me my week-long lay-in notices for the past couple of months, Janine took the time to review my file, to see the notes about my needing an MRI, and to ask me how much pain I was in.

"What's with all these week-long lay-in notices I see in your file? Nobody gets MRI's around here. I'm going to ask the doctor to issue you a two-month lay-in notice."

"Thanks so much!"

She then went and not only had the doctor sign a two-month lay-in notice for me, but also made two extra copies for me: one for our dorm unit manager, and one for Officer Nimrod.

When she returned with the three copies of my lay-in notice, I couldn't resist teasing her about the signs I'd seen all over the camp claiming that Taft's motto was "BIONIC", which stood for "Believe It Or Not I Care."

"Hey Janine. Believe it or not, I know you care!"

To which she replied: "That's because I refuse to follow the camp's true motto, which is "BIONICAL", which means "Believe It Or Not I Care A Little."

Janine knew I was faking the severity of my injury, too. She just didn't want to see my soul get injured any more than it already had.

One person who clearly didn't give a shit if he fucked up my soul, by contrast, was Joseph.

83

CHAPTER 16

BEGINNING OF THE END IN JOSEPH WORLD

Fall of 2007-Fall of 2009

During my first decade as a lawyer, I'd spent ninety percent of my time fighting to save the lives of my immigration clients in court. During my time with Joseph, I would end up spending ninety percent of my time fighting to achieve better standards of living for his mostly employment-based immigrant clients.

Then one day, upon my return from vacation in the fall of 2007, Joseph calmly informed me that he'd been falsely accused of immigration fraud by the Feds, and that he'd been under investigation for the past several months. My jaw dropped as he went on to tell me that none of his Chinese clients had played along with the Feds, but now a young, thin, nervous Polish client named Derek, who had also been pressured by the Feds, was insisting on a meeting with us both.

Joseph had always called me "The Fireman" for my ability to remain cool in a crisis. This meeting sounded like it could well be my finest hour. I pictured Joseph waiting in a building, alone. I then pictured the Feds pouring gasoline all over Derek, sending him off to this meeting, and then lighting a match behind him to try to burn down the consulting business Joseph had worked so hard for the past sixteen years to build up.

"Why does this client need to meet with me?" I asked.

"Because the Feds are leaning on him hard to lie and falsely accuse me of fraud, and he needs you to reassure him that he won't get in any trouble if he refuses to do so."

I drove towards the Barnes & Noble bookstore in Irvine, closest to where Derek lived. Now you're in, Kelly Darwin, I said to myself. Now you're in.

By the time I arrived at the bookstore, Joseph and Derek had already ordered coffee and were sitting talking. I strolled in, wearing my wrinkled suit and a baseball cap, and ordered an ice water.

"The Feds don't believe I'm really working for my sponsoring employer. They're threatening to throw me in prison if I don't admit that I'm not," Derek began. All the paperwork I'd reviewed clearly confirmed that Derek was working for his sponsoring employer.

"Don't let them intimidate you," I replied. "They do this sort of thing all the time, hoping you'll crack."

The conversation continued for a while longer. Derek seemed way too nervous. Joseph seemed way too reassuring. Something seemed off. I was still unsure of the details of Joseph's arrangement with Derek, as I'd always been a big picture guy, so I was letting Joseph act like a general planning a battle, since that's what he seemed to want.

Joseph's telling me that he's being falsely accused of immigration fraud. But now Joseph's telling Derek he'd better clean up his records or else? This is how you defend yourself against false charges of fraud? These two are professionals? Now I couldn't leave. I needed to stay to see how this all played out.

"Okay, Derek," says Joseph. "Here's your chance to prove to the Feds that you didn't do what you did."

I'd been a little scared when they first started talking together. Now I'm getting even more scared, and mad too. I don't understand what Joseph just said to Derek. I don't know if I'm stupid or just scared, but it burns my ass that Derek understood the things Joseph said, and I couldn't. Like what the hell did Joseph mean by "you didn't do what you did"?

The longer I listened to Joseph and Derek talk, the more my head started to throb.

You and me are parting ways real soon! I thought to myself as soon as the meeting finally ended. My hand holding the ice water was shaking, but Joseph didn't notice. I clenched my teeth together to hide the quiver in my chin. Sweating. Cold. Lightheaded. Panicked. But I couldn't leave. Joseph and I had worked together for too long. I couldn't just abandon ship now. Just as I'd never been able to shake loose from my mom, so deep was my fear of her abandoning me, I couldn't shake loose from Joseph now.

I felt myself go limp after a few moments had passed. I knew I couldn't continue working with Joseph on Derek's case. Or maybe any case.

After the meeting ended, my stomach was in knots. Joseph had been changing stories. The way his story suddenly shifted from one moment to the next, as suddenly Joseph went from being falsely accused of immigration fraud to maybe having lied a little on Derek's case. That line about not having done what you did was the tell. As a lawyer, I'd always known that framing was an essential skill. But there was a world of difference between framing and lying. Fucking liars, that's what Joseph and Derek were.

At least the meeting had finally ended. I could start breathing again.

I confronted Joseph immediately after the meeting. "What the hell was going on in there just now?"

"Well, Derek told me when we first got to the coffee shop, before you showed up, that he hadn't been working as many hours as we'd told Immigration he was, but he now knows he's got to work full-time or his case will be denied."

"And you decided to tell me this *after* our meeting with him!"

This was the first time in the sixteen years I'd known Joseph, and in the eight years we'd worked together, that he'd ever admitted having lied to me. It's also the first time I'd noticed something off. Joseph and his wife May had come to our wedding, fifteen years earlier. We'd been to barbeques at their home and had gotten to know their three kids. We considered him a friend, just as they considered us to be friends.

Suddenly Joseph, who'd been my eight-year long "safe harbor", didn't seem so safe anymore.

I called my civil litigator friend Tom, whom I'd befriended while working with Ron, and asked for his advice.

"Joseph just told me that he's been under investigation by the Feds for months. He claims he's being falsely accused of immigration fraud, but after a meeting with a client just now, he admitted to me that the client has been lying to the Feds. What the fuck do I do now?" I began.

"You get the hell out of there, my friend. Are any of your immigration lawyer friends hiring? If that's not an option, then at least quit being 'of counsel' to him. Set up your own office, and don't let him anywhere near it, as at least that way you can ensure that all the cases you handle are clean."

"Thanks, Tom. I will."

"Word to the wise, Kel. I don't care how long you've known Joseph, or how much you think he cares about you. The Feds don't care about him, they're looking for the big fish. Joseph's just a consultant, but you're the lawyer here—the big fish they're looking for. If this shit really hits the fan, Joseph will throw you under the bus like roadkill."

My hands were sweating as I shakily hung up the phone.

I called up every immigration lawyer friend I could think of, to see if anyone was hiring. My friend and fellow Pepperdine alum, Susan Hill, called me in for an interview. She could offer me a job, she said, but her firm wouldn't be able to absorb all of Joseph's existing clients as well. I knew I could no longer trust Joseph, but I still felt a duty to his remaining clients, who had put their trust in me for so many years now.

After that meeting with Derek, after Tom's warning about the dangers of sticking around, I still could have cut Joseph loose. I could have made up some excuse. I could have weaseled out by claiming that the job offer from Susan was just too good to pass up. But I didn't.

When I told Joseph I wanted to go work with Susan, he hastily arranged a meeting with Ellen, a young Hong Kong-born immigrant who had previously worked as our paralegal. Joseph was desperate enough to do whatever he could to hold on to me, but I couldn't see that.

"You can't just abandon our clients, Kel," Joseph pleaded. "Ellen has agreed to work as your office manager in your new office."

"And you will have no contact with any of the clients in my new office?"

"None. Ellen will be your office manager, and I will not be involved at all."

"Well, Susan says she wouldn't be able to absorb all of our clients, so I guess this arrangement will have to do, as I can't just leave them twisting in the wind."

I decided that I was going to leave Joseph as soon as I possibly could. Set up my own office. Take over all of Joseph's clients, not just those I'd already worked with. Make sure every case was clean. But I was going to leave with Joseph's clients. He owed me that much at least.

"There's just one condition," Joseph continued. The dazzling sunlight sliced through the designer blinds to my right, stabbing the coffin-grey office wall to my left. I was sitting across from Joseph. He had a bunch of spreadsheets in front of him. He was explaining to me how much his consulting business had made over the past several years. How much my projected revenues should be for my new firm, which would be taking on all his current clients. My eyes glazed over as he droned on, until I heard him say, "Based on these projected revenue figures, you should have no problem paying me ten grand a month, as that's how much my mortgage is."

"Really? That's how much we pay for our mortgage for a year," I said, swallowing hard.

I felt trapped, as I knew that without his clients, I'd have no revenues.

"Also, the clients I've worked so hard to pass on to you are worth it. I ran the numbers, and we've been averaging about six hundred clients per year. So at roughly two grand per case, that's $1.2 million in annual gross revenues. You'll only have to pay me ten percent of that, and that way, within about four years, you'll have sufficiently compensated me for handing over all my clients to you, I figure."

"Wait, give me a moment, will you. That's a lot of numbers to process." I sank back in my chair. Thinking of the fifteen grand a month I'd be conceivably making in about four years' time didn't help. Because I couldn't imagine fifteen grand a month. It was too much. It was just a wildly inconceivable amount. I think about Linda, with all her health issues, no longer having to work full-time. I think about moving out of our cluttered condo and finally having bookshelves for all my books and a place for all of Linda's music stuff. I think about paying off the ten-year lease on my car. Being able to enjoy the fourth-floor corner office view of the mountains that Joseph now savors. Having other people work for me, instead of always working for other people.

"And what would Ellen be doing as my new office manager?"

"She'll be doing the books, keeping track of payroll, and managing the case files. All the stuff I used to do. You should pay her five grand a month for that."

Wow, I thought, she'd be making as much as I was. And I'd been a lawyer for almost twenty years already.

"And what will you be doing?"

"I've got plans for after I start turning over my clients to you. I've been talking to some of those pastors we were planning on preparing religious worker cases for. They suggested, and I agreed, that I should go to seminary and become a minister."

"Really? Here all these years I've thought that helping immigrants was my ministry."

"Not me, man. You can keep helping them as long as you like. For me, though, helping immigrants was just a temporary gig, on my way to my true calling as a minister of the gospel."

I had no idea he felt that way. Here I'd thought all along we were both ministering to immigrants together. How wrong I'd been.

"And even with this fraud investigation hanging over your head, you don't think there'll be a drop in revenues?"

"Hell no. I've now managed to clean up the few minor issues that one client had."

He's getting ready to screw me over again, I thought to myself. But I said nothing. I couldn't abandon our clients. Mom had always said "look how much I've sacrificed for you". I guessed it must be my turn to do some sacrificing.

My hands became clammy when I remembered Tom's warning that Joseph would throw me under the bus like roadkill if the shit ever really hit the fan.

But it was stupid to think like that. There was no real risk to me. I was, after all, nothing more than Joseph's fireman. If the Feds ever did decide to take Joseph down, I should still be able to walk away clean.

I'd done nothing wrong. But had Joseph? That was something I just couldn't allow myself to consider.

I think, shoot, maybe I pay him ten grand a month for the next four years. Then all his clients will be mine, and I can triple my salary by paying myself that extra ten grand a month out of the firm's revenues.

Linda had been the primary breadwinner our entire married life. But she'd gotten injured at work, and now suffered from fibromyalgia and multiple chemical sensitivity as a result. And she'd had breast cancer two years earlier. She couldn't keep working forever. Maybe I could even start treating Linda to a few of the finer things, even though she'd taken a vow of poverty when she'd been in a Christian community in her younger years. A better place to live than this cramped Culver City condo we'd been living in for the past fifteen years. Maybe not Joseph's one and half million-dollar mansion in the West Covina hills, but an upgrade at least. But now I was dreaming, and I knew it. Getting past my "one year at a time" mantra.

I stopped and thought about the coming year. It was December 4th. A month from now it would be 2008. Set up my own office this month, start paying Joseph ten grand a month. If the revenue figures held up like Joseph seemed confident they would, I'd keep the arrangement going on long enough for me to buy Joseph out. I would then cut Joseph loose and start making real money. The kind of money that would mean Linda could finally start working fewer hours, or possibly not even have to work. God knows she deserved at least that.

"Okay," I say. "I'll pay you the ten grand a month." I was surprised by the fire that flashed in Joseph's brown eyes, and the wide triumphant smile, and the excited chuckle that burst forth. I couldn't understand the jubilation, but then I didn't understand that I could have simply turned Joseph down and gone to work for Susan instead. I was so desperate not to abandon our clients, nor to be abandoned by Joseph, that I could not see that I was abandoning myself by staying on.

I accepted his demand to pay him ten grand a month, and thought, I'm supposed to take over his clients, and in just a few short years, I'll be able to do just that. It's just gotta be. It's just meant to be. And I started making those payments. For twenty-two months. To my destiny.

Never mind that this was more than double what I was paying myself. Never mind that I was agreeing to pay Ellen, my new office manager, at least as much as, and maybe more than, I could afford to pay myself.

Now it occurred to me that while I was setting up my own office, I really hadn't cut Joseph loose. I'd just moved him into the shadows. And nothing had been put into writing. God, was I naïve.

The Joseph I knew was not a fraudster. With me he was caring and concerned, as committed to fighting for our immigrant clients as I was. What Joseph held for me was primal. His self-assurance, coupled with his repeatedly calling me "the fireman", had the effect of making me feel fathered again. I needed to be needed, and Joseph's need for me was the drug I craved.

When I returned to our condo after this conversation with Joseph, I cursed the clutter. I was sick to death of our crowded condo. I wanted the wide-open spaces of a place like Joseph's, with his grand piano in the living room. Bookshelves for all my books, instead of having them scattered all over the floor, where I could, and often did, trip over them. A music room for all of Linda's music stuff. But then I remembered that sleepless first semester at Pepperdine Law School. Strung out on sleeping pills. Terrified that I might never sleep again. Better a cluttered condo than a sleepless dorm room.

For the next two years, beginning just before Christmas in 2007, I set up and ran my own immigration law office, with Ellen as my office manager, and as far as I knew handled nothing but clean cases. Joseph stayed the hell away, as promised. Still, Joseph's demand for those monthly payments seemed to grow more insistent over time, to the point where, when profits dipped, I had to take out a business loan to keep paying him as promised.

His plans to "go to seminary to become a minister", however, seemed to be in a state of perpetual postponement.

And when I ended up being arrested at LAX twenty-two months later, I reflected bitterly on the fact that while I may have misguidedly thought I was paying ten grand a month for a "four years to financial freedom" card, all I was really buying was a front row seat for my own execution.

Only after my arrest would one of the many surprises of discovery turn out to be that Derek had been telling the Feds the truth about Joseph all along. I had been unable to abandon Joseph's clients who'd put their faith in me, however, as I was haunted by a time that I'd been unable to stand up for a friend who'd trusted me. I'd been ten at the time, when three or four hulking seventh graders approached me on the schoolyard moments after our release from captivity. They wanted me to pile on a weaker kid with them, a kid who was a friend of mine. And because I was so afraid, I did it, leading them to my friend Malcolm, then watching helplessly as they tied him to a tree, avoiding his hurt terror when I walked away. All I cared about was that I was no longer the scrawniest kid in my class, and at least those hulking seventh graders had noticed me. Malcolm would later forgive me for this, but for decades I'd been unable to forgive myself.

Four decades later, my role in betraying Malcolm that day still haunted me. That fall afternoon, I was choosing sides. I would be an insider. I would be like Robbie Bartram, who'd bullied me. Like those seventh graders.

In the fall of 2009, I would end up becoming a literal prisoner in a much more terrifying house of fear. I would be forced to try and untie Writer Kel from that tree, in the desperate hope that he might be able to remind me once again how to be a spy, rather than a prisoner, there. That literal house of fear would end up triggering flashbacks to both my, and my adoptive mom's, childhood houses of fear.

CHAPTER 17

FROM THE PRICE OF POSTAGE
TO THE DEATH OF TICO

August 2013

"Mom's pissed. She says you haven't written to thank her yet for the book she sent you last week."

My sister's email glared at me from the prison computer screen during my half hour of daily email access.

My sister Shauna was referring to our adoptive mom, Pat. She was my third mom. There was also my foster mom Grace, now a hundred and two years old and no longer in need of updates from the son with whom she'd reunited about a dozen years earlier. In fact, after having spent the first eleven months of my life in her care, I figured it was best that she not discover that the only one of her eleven foster kids to have reunited with her was now spending almost as long in federal prison – ten months – as he'd spent being cared for by her.

And then there was my birthmother, Adele. Given that she'd just been a kid herself when she'd gotten pregnant with me, she was young enough to be able to check my Facebook page for the frequent status updates my film-maker friend Jason was posting for me, or she could email me if she wanted a more personalized update.

But Pat was old school. No email, no social media in her world. Just good old-fashioned snail mail. And besides, my sister's email had gone on to remind me, our mom had written two letters a week to her mom until the week she died. Wow. How was I ever going to compete with that?

It reminded of the film I'd seen a few years back about John Lennon's childhood called *Nowhere Boy*. Near the end of that film, after John Lennon had suffered the tragic deaths of both his adoptive dad and birthmother, he called his adoptive mom every week until the week he died.

And so I emailed my sister back and explained that I was so poor that I could not even afford to pay for the stamps to send mom a letter of thanks. This was private prison at its finest. They were feeding us for twenty-five cents a day. That meant rice and beans and precious little else. As a result, I was forced to spend my monthly limit in commissary buying things like bread, tuna, avocado, fruits, vegetables, granola, and raw almonds. Okay, and white chocolate raspberry truffle ice cream, just to make sure I was eating at least one item on the "foods most likely to kill you" list from our mandatory health and nutrition class. But hey, since I hadn't been allowed to work out ever since I'd injured my Achilles, my only hope of not gaining fifty pounds during my stay was to buy all the food I could from commissary.

I felt bad, though. So I wrote mom a letter. I lied to her, like I'd spent my life doing. I told her that this prison was a lot like summer camp. Except there was no kayaking. And a lot more stupid rules to follow. And that even if I didn't end up getting my degree in Ministry, I was fine with that. I told her I thought I'd make a much better poetry therapist than a minister or chaplain anyways.

My sister felt bad, too. She sent me money for my commissary account so I could afford to buy stamps. Her timing was off, though, as she sent the money one day too soon. The day it landed in my account, I was scheduled for my "team meeting". Apparently, there's no I, nor postage stamps for that matter, in team. At my team meeting, I was informed that the money which had just arrived from my sister was now being re-routed from my commissary account to pay for my lawyer-upgraded "special assessment" from the court. I realized there'd be no ice cream this month, or mom would never get that letter I wrote.

When I was on the outside, I would rarely take the Neurontin I'd been prescribed for my Chronic Regional Pain Syndrome (CRPS), also known as Reflex Sympathetic Dystrophy (RSD), except for right before going to sleep. I'd been afflicted with these ailments ever since a car crash, where I'd been blindsided by a red-light runner, had left me with severe nerve damage in my neck, which affected my right arm.

But the severity of those injuries from that car crash hadn't kept me from driving on the outside, as in a city like Los Angeles, driving is about as essential as breathing if I'd wanted to keep working, which I needed to do to try to avoid bankruptcy. But since Neurontin's side effects include drowsiness, that was something I could ill-afford with all the driving I had to do.

But now that I'd self-surrendered, there'd be no more driving for me. And in a place like Taft, I was loving Neurontin's other side-effects, like vivid sleep-time and even lucid dreaming, as anything was an improvement over my day-to-day reality. My drug lords became a rotating series of nurses at the medical office. There was Nurse Janine, the one fully human nurse, who was truly a humane presence in an inhumane place. And then there were the rest: a series of robot nurses who had been much more successfully programmed to eliminate emotional involvement with the inmates. My daily fixes were at 7 am, noon, and 5 pm. And those fixes helped me escape, however briefly, from the bleak programming of my daily existence.

Every evening, I leaned back into the thrashed green exercise mat from the exercise room, which now served as all the furnishings I needed for my fully furnished artists and Principled Rebels' Clubhouse/tree-house/office (aka the dugout next to the baseball diamond) at Taft Federal Prison. I stretched out my legs onto the once green but now mostly unpainted wooden "desk", defining the term rather loosely. I gazed through the chain link fence, which shielded me during the day from overthrown pitches and missed throws to the plate, at the gorgeous moon blazing like the eye of God. The Tower of Babel-like floodlights surrounding the baseball diamond couldn't compete with the glorious radiance of the moonlight.

If this isn't great, I don't know what is.

In my School of Ministry classes, I kept getting consistently high grades on my essays from inmate instructor Stone, but consistently low grades from inmate instructor Mike. I figured he was having trouble reading my scrawling cursive, so I rewrote my essays for him in block letters, and still got low grades. I then asked if we could discuss my grades and he invited me over to his dorm to do so.

Once we arrived at Mike's cube, his opening statement helped me better understand how this whole misunderstanding had arisen.

"You're a lawyer, right?" Mike began. I knew Mike was, too.

"Hell, no," I replied. "I'm an artist who played the role of a lawyer just a little too long."

Unable to shake this misconception, Mike persisted in this line of questioning. He showed me one of his essays, and said, "Why can't you write like this?"

"Because that looks like a legal brief," I said. "I only wrote like that because I had to, in order to save my clients. Since I no longer have any clients, I can only write for two audiences: God, and myself. Maybe for a handful of others. But I sure don't have any clients to write for."

I watched as Mike's face softened into a grin, and we proceeded to have our first truly human conversation since we'd met some twelve weeks earlier. Mike promised me I'd be receiving my amended grades soon. Humanity had won.

The next day, as my monthly visit with Linda was drawing to a close, I noticed a young Mexican boy, who'd been visiting his father that same day, returning the game Aggravation before his departure. I asked him and his older brother if they'd enjoyed playing the game with their father that day.

"Yeah, we loved it!" they said in unison.

"Did you know that my dad invented that game? We still have the original round wooden board back home in Canada."

"Really?" the younger brother said. "We used to play it on a square wooden board back home in Mexico."

A game that Pops had created and played for fun on a round wooden board in Canada became something that a generation of Mexican kids had grown up playing for fun on a square wooden board. Meanwhile, here in the States, some enterprising American named Harry First submitted a patent application for the same game about a year before I was born, and so a generation of American kids grew up playing the patented, plastic version of it.

A week later, Tico died. He was only in his forties. He was walking around the track when he collapsed. An announcement boomed over the prison complex, "Man down!" and we were all hustled back to our dorms. Several of my dormmates who'd been walking on the track when it happened said that his face had already turned blue by the time they were ordered to leave the area.

The one human nurse in the facility, Nurse Janine, had been on duty that day and was first on the scene. All attempts to revive Tico had failed. Half an hour later, an ambulance crept slowly into the compound, and, once Tico's body had been loaded on board, slipped slowly out of the compound. We all watched from our dorm in stunned silence.

What happened next was even more surreal. The robots attempted to assure us all that Tico had not died, but was on life-support at the hospital.

Nurse Janine was on pill call that day. When I went for my 5 pm fix of Neurontin, Nurse Janine was still sobbing softly, and told me that she'd done all that she could, but had been unable to save Tico.

The next day, Nurse Janine was gone, as she'd been a little too human to keep toeing the party line about Tico not having died in prison.

We learned later that one of the other nurses had given Tico the wrong heart meds, and so the prison could never publicly acknowledge that he had died while in their care. Nurse Janine had been the scapegoat to try to keep that secret safe. Similarly, the Feds could never admit that Joseph had acted alone, or perhaps in concert with his wife, in orchestrating his immigrant fraud scheme, as they'd spent too much money on their investigation, and so I became the scapegoat to try to keep that secret safe.

CHAPTER 18

RETURN TO THE CRIME SCENE

October 26, 2009

Upon my release on bond from the Metropolitan Detention Center on Friday, which would at least enable me to fight my case from outside those prison walls, I got a chance to go onstage with U2 at the Rose Bowl as an Amnesty International volunteer less than forty-eight hours later, to raise awareness about the plight of Aung San Suu Kyi, who had been wrongfully detained in Burma for the past two decades. The following morning, reality returned with a vengeance.

I pulled into the parking lot of TGI Friday's restaurant in West Covina, next to the Chase Bank building my office was in. My stomach churned. My tension eased as I saw Michael A. pull in next to me.

We walked towards the building together, and, just as we were about to go in, I saw Craig, a tall, lanky, African American, exiting the bank on his way to his car. Craig, my teller at Chase, had become a good friend over the years.

Craig smiled broadly and waved us over. He'd responded to my last Facebook posting eleven days earlier, when I'd learned that my office had been raided. The day I'd posted a rather cryptic message asking for prayer.

"Damn, it's good to see you again, Kel," he said, and gave me a hug. "When those ICE agents swarmed your office, and then I read your Facebook post, I was really worried."

"Thanks, Craig. This is my lawyer, Michael, who's going to help me fight my case."

Craig shook Michael's hand firmly.

"Fight like hell, man!" Craig said and headed off to his car.

Michael and I entered the building and took the elevator to the fifth floor. My hands shook as I fumbled with the key to my office door.

Nothing could have prepared me for the devastation. Files in manila folders, files spilling out of boxes, half-empty file cabinets, loose papers, and trash, including a stray orange, were strewn about everywhere. I slumped down in a chair in the reception area, breathing heavily, afraid I might faint.

Michael came in behind me, and his eyes widened as he surveyed the scene. He sat down across from me.

"A good place to start would be to see what mail arrived during your absence," he began.

I made my way gingerly over to the receptionist's desk, where all the mail had been neatly stacked, and began flipping through it.

"Anything in particular I should be looking for?"

"Be on the lookout for mail from clients who might be part of the Feds' case against you. From now on, pass any potentially case-related mail to me, unopened. That way the Feds can't accuse you of trying to tamper with potential witnesses."

"I have no idea which clients Joseph might have sold those fake work visas to."

Michael reached down into his battered black briefcase, pulled out an inch-thick document, and handed it to me.

"That's a copy of your indictment. I'm still reviewing it myself. Included is a list of both the shell companies Joseph set up, and the clients who paid him extra to not have to work for those companies."

As I flipped through the weighty document, my hands trembled. Joseph's fraud had been both wide-ranging and well-hidden.

"Oh, wow." I let out a low whistle. "He was quite the operator." I see that Derek's case was Joseph's eighty-fifth fraudulent case while I was of counsel to him. It was the last fraudulent case he ever prepared. He hadn't committed any fraud when we'd started working together eight years earlier, but only during the past five years had he gotten greedy and started engaging in fraud.

I leafed through the mail a second time, this time much more deliberately. I searched specifically for mail addressed to any listed companies, or from any listed clients.

"Here's one," I said. "It's a letter from Derek's wife. Derek is the Polish client who insisted on meeting with Joseph and I at that Barnes & Noble bookstore. It was after that meeting I first began to suspect that Joseph might have been lying to me about the Feds having falsely accused him of fraud."

"Ok," Michael said. "I'll hold on to that for you. Oh, and about that meeting with Joseph and Derek…"

"Yeah?" I looked up at Michael from behind the pile of mail.

"You do know that Derek was wearing a wire, right?"

"Hell, no. Was he really?"

"Afraid so."

"Well, that would explain a few things. Like that newspaper article you showed me the other day which said that one of the applicants had recorded a conversation with Joseph and me, and that during that conversation I encouraged one of the cooperating witnesses to lie to the investigators. What the fuck did they mean by that?"

"Well, Kel, I've watched the video and listened to the audio from the bookstore, and it doesn't look good."

"How does it look?"

"It looks like you are telling Derek, the cooperating witness who's been lying to the Feds, not to be intimidated by them. The prosecutor is going to say that you were encouraging him to lie."

I stared into Michael's eyes. "But how could I be encouraging Derek to lie? I thought that Derek had been telling the Feds the truth, but that the Feds had been trying to intimidate Derek into lying about Joseph to back up their false accusations."

Michael looked away.

"And you believed Joseph?"

"Hell, yeah. We'd been friends for twenty years, and as far as I knew, he'd never lied to me before. Not only that, but I believed him to the point that I paid him ten grand a month for the next twenty-two months for his clients, as they were the only clients I had for the new firm I'd set up."

"There's a first time for everything, I suppose. But here's another painful truth: juries hate lawyers. If the Feds have a lawyer on tape looking like he's encouraging a client to lie, the jury's going to buy it."

I sank lower in my chair. "But can't you question the jurors to try to weed out the most biased ones?"

Michael exhaled softly. "In state court, yes, as lawyers there can freely question prospective jurors through a process called *voir dire*. It's one of my greatest gifts. But it can't be used in federal court. All we can do is submit questions for the prospective jurors to the judge. We can't ask any follow-up questions."

"So what does that mean, Michael? Is there any hope for me?"

"Not a lot. Going to court would be too high risk. Our best hope will be to try convince your prosecutor that you had no idea what Joseph was doing and you didn't profit from it, and hope to God she believes us and offers you a decent plea deal."

"Well, both of those things are true. Hopefully we can do just that."

Michael nodded encouragingly, and then turned and made his way out of the office.

I waded through the scattered files, papers and trash, nearly tripping over the discarded orange, and wearily sat down at my desk.

Was my twenty year career as an immigration lawyer about to end? Why had I trusted Joseph so much?

All I could do for now was to take Michael's advice and keep fighting for the handful of clients I had left. I'd also have to help Michael fight the Feds for a plea deal that would hopefully save me from disbarment and spending more time behind bars. What would that plea deal look like? House arrest? Money? If we could plead the felonies down to a misdemeanor like negligence, for example, the worst I'd be looking at would likely be some type of fine and/or probation, and possibly a temporary suspension of my law license.

I was terrified. I needed Michael to save Lawyer Kel from annihilation. But nearly four decades earlier, I'd also been terrified, and had needed to be a good Christian to save me from the fear that my adoptive mom might abandon me. Later, I'd been terrified that Joseph would abandon me. If only I'd been aware of how much I'd abandoned myself in response to those fears.

CHAPTER 19

FROM KEL-DAR DANCING TO PRISON BAPTISM TO INSPIRING ZACHARY

August 2013

Having read about twenty-five science fiction novels during my first few months in prison, I'd begun writing my own sci-fi novel, fleshing out its universe out of my own prison experience—which was good for something it turned out. There was Kel-Dar, my sci-fi alter ego, robots (almost all the prison staff), humans (those of us who got ratted on), and humanoid robots (rats and other ass-kissing inmates). Severin Stone was one of the humans, and had helped me win a small victory over the robots the week before. But I wasn't just creating sci-fi out of my experiences, sometimes the experiences would come to me.

For example, that Sunday's prison chapel service. The third Sunday of every month, this electrifying gospel group named The Watkins Family would perform.

Severin introduced The Watkins Family's blues gospel show with a reminder that even King David had "played the fool" before God, including the time he danced naked in front of the Ark of the Covenant and embarrassed his wife by doing so. I took Severin's advice to heart, as I'd always felt like church should be at least as religious an experience as a U2 concert. Before long I was dancing in the aisles with my cane. Kel-Dar, who as a child had been nicknamed Special K, had finally made an appearance.

Once the blues/gospel jam was done, a minister from the same church as The Watkins Family took the stage. He told us he'd decided to scrap his pre-planned message for a "word from the Lord' he'd just received. He told us that somebody who was quite young here in our prison camp was in grave physical and spiritual danger, as he was harboring a lot of bitterness and resentment, and that something very serious might happen to him physically within the next day. We were all worried, but none of us had any idea who it might be. Once I got back to my dorm, I told several of my friends about this word of warning.

* * * * *

I would later learn that a few hours after that service, my good friend "Goose," whom I'd volunteered with during my first month in the Native American Garden, and who was in a different dorm from mine, had come over to our dorm complaining of severe stomach pain. He'd asked a couple of my friends for help, and they'd remembered what I'd told them I'd just heard in chapel and figured it might have been a warning about Goose. They'd immediately called the staff to take Goose to emergency. The only treatment he'd been given for this latest flare up of his pancreatic cysts was an ultrasound, as that is a three or four hundred dollar test, rather than what he's supposed to be given every six months, which is a CT scan, a three or four thousand dollar test. He had not been given a CT scan in over a year.

Goose's bitterness and resentment was therefore clearly understandable. I was inspired by my friend Red to reach out to Goose and tried to help him get the CT scan he so desperately needed, before his precancerous pancreatic cysts turned cancerous. Red had taken his case to trial and lost, and so had devoted his time in prison to helping his fellow inmates fight their cases. I had so far failed to get an MRI for my Achilles injury, but in my failures had learned a few things about the system that would hopefully help Goose get his much more critically needed CT scan. His dormmate Severin prayed over him several times in the middle of the night over the next few weeks. When I dropped in on him several weeks later to drop off some information about an upcoming sweat-lodge ceremony Goose was planning, I noticed he was reading a little pamphlet called "Our Daily Bread", which is a book of daily

Christian devotions. I smiled to myself, as it seemed that Goose was finally allowing himself to be open to the possibility that there might just be a God who loves him after all.

* * * * *

Unaware of that at the time however, both Brandon and I were trying to figure out who the pastor might have been referring to. Now stocky, blond-haired Brandon was in his early twenties, was just getting started on a ten-year sentence for a non-violent drug offense, and was the most spiritual guy I knew in our dorm, with a daily meditation practice. Both Brandon and I had recently met the dark-haired, wiry Zachary, another kid in his early twenties, who'd just transferred in from another facility, and who was also near the start of a ten-year bid for a non-violent drug crime.

"Do you think the pastor might have been talking about Zachary?" Brandon asked me when we returned to our dorm after chapel that night.

"Yeah, maybe," I said. "When I talked with him in the cafeteria the other day, he really seemed to be in a dark place, spiritually."

"Yeah, that's what I thought too," said Brandon.

"I'll see if I can go talk with him tomorrow," I said.

Since we were in the upstairs Dorm C, and Zachary was right beneath us in the downstairs Dorm A, I had to wait until we were released from lockdown the next morning before I could try to find him. After asking around his fellow dormmates as to where he might be, I finally found him in the Dorm A quiet room.

"Hey, Zachary, I'm taking this Biblical Counseling Class right now, and one of our homework assignments is to do a mock intake interview with somebody. Would it be okay if I ask you a few questions about your-self, as though I were your therapist and you were my patient?"

"Sure, fire away."

"Which parent would you say you were closest to when you were growing up, your mom or your dad?"

"Well, my mom left home when I was six years old and didn't come back until I was sixteen. I would have to say my dad, since I barely know my mom."

And suddenly it struck me. Zachary and I were like twin sons of different mothers. Our abandonment fears may have sprung from different sources, mine from the first year of my life spent in a foster home before I was adopted, and from losing Pops, my adoptive dad, to a permanent head injury when I was twenty five, and his from a mom who disappeared from his life for a decade of his childhood, but our fears were very much the same.

I'd written three poetry collections over a two-year period to try to give voice to, and begin to heal from, some of my abandonment fears, and had brought those with me to prison.

"Wow," I told Zachary. "You and I've got a lot in common. Let me go get something from my dorm. I'll be right back."

And with that I went upstairs and grabbed my first poetry volume and brought it back downstairs.

"Here," I said. "This is the first book of poetry I wrote to try to work through some of my abandonment fears. Take a look through it and let me know if any of the poems resonate for you."

"Cool, thanks!" he replied.

I ran into him again in the cafeteria a few days later.

"So did you get a chance to read any of those poems yet?" I began.

"Hell, yeah," he said, handing me back the book with several of the pages dog-eared. "I highlighted all the ones that really got me."

I looked more closely at the book he'd returned after I went back to my dorm, and was thrilled to see that he'd highlighted a dozen of the poems. I went over to the prison library and made copies of the ones he'd highlighted and gave him the copies and promised him that I would leave the book with him when it came time for my release.

I'd spent much of my life trying to save others to try to avoid facing my own pain. At least on this occasion it had been my willingness to try to work through some of my own pain that had enabled me to be there for Zachary as he was working his way through his.

A few weeks after I'd made copies of the poems for him, as I was sitting next to Zachary in chapel, I was telling him about how I'd gotten my final exam grades for my first eight weeks of the Christian School of Ministry classes, but that I hadn't received a grade for my essay yet. I was then handed a note from the chaplains that said, *"We hereby regretfully inform you that because you have recently changed your religious affiliation from Protestant to Native American, it seems that you no longer agree with the Chaplains College Statement of Faith and the doctrinal statement it represents. Consequently, you are no longer eligible to continue in the Associate Degree program, as you are not in compliance with the policies of the college."*

I sat for a moment in stunned disbelief.

"Hey, Zach, check this out. The robots say I recently changed my religious affiliation to Native American."

"When did you change it?"

"Almost four months ago, right after I got here, as it was the only way I could be a volunteer in the Native American Garden. And then they say I must no longer agree with the Christian statement of faith and doctrinal statement."

"Yeah, so do you?"

"Of course. I just read up on Native American spirituality for that sweat lodge we're planning, and I didn't see anything inconsistent with Christianity. And besides, my adoptive dad is part Metis."

"Then you were just honoring your father, right?"

"You bet."

I handed Zachary the note.

As Zachary was reading the note for himself, I happened to notice in the chapel bulletin that they were going to be having baptisms the following weekend.

"Look, man, if they're saying I'm no longer a Christian, I'd better get re-baptized next weekend and prove them wrong!" I said.

"I want a front row seat for that, dude!" replied Zachary.

Zachary did come and watch me get re-baptized that next weekend. I was wearing my grey khaki prison shorts as about a dozen of us huddled together in the middle of the soccer field. *I wonder what they're going to baptize us in?* I thought to myself. Unlike Catholics, who perform infant baptism where the baby just gets sprinkled with water, we Protestants go in for full-immersion baptism. Growing up in the Alliance Church in Victoria, the baptismal tank at the front of the church looked kind of like an oversized bathtub. That was probably partly why I waited until I moved down to LA before getting baptized for the first time, as that way I was able to get baptized in the ocean down at Venice Beach.

Suddenly, off in the distance, we saw a vision of a faded blue-green dumpster being wheeled in our direction. It kicked up a cloud of dust as several of our fellow inmates shepherded it across the desert sand.

Once it arrived, I peered inside, but soon wished I hadn't. I noticed a dead rat floating amongst some rancid potatoes and putrid carrots along the surface, and near the bottom a layer of what appeared to have been leftover milk, which had since turned to cheese in the desert heat. One of my fellow inmates held his nose and removed the rat by its tail.

When it was my turn, I crept up towards the dumpster, climbed up the makeshift ladder of cardboard placed beside it, and slid inside. The slimy lukewarm water wasn't so bad, but my feet squishing in the spongy layer along the bottom made it hard for me to concentrate on what my friend Severin was saying as he first dunked me below the surface and then raised my head back up out of the water.

"Do you intend to be Christ's faithful disciple, trusting his promises, obeying his word, honoring his church, and showing his love, as long as you live?" I managed to hear him say.

"Sure," I replied. *As long as I can get unstuck from this quicksand,* I thought to myself.

"I baptize you in the name of the Father, the Son, and the Holy Spirit. Amen."

"Amen!" I echoed. I struggled to free myself, and then called Severin, whose nickname was Stone, back over.

"Hey Stone, it seems I'm a little stuck here." I gave him my right hand, he pulled, and I finally managed to yank both my feet free. I descended the makeshift staircase, my teeth chattering in the early morning breeze.

The very same pastor who'd suspended and removed me from the Christian School of Ministry would end up being the one to sign my baptismal certificate. Despite my re-baptism, I was never reinstated into the Associate Degree program, as my "change of religion" was apparently an irrevocable, unforgiveable sin. I continued to take all the School of Ministry classes that I possibly could, despite not receiving any grades or credit for them. The baptism itself had been more than memorable enough for me to not even care. They could take away any external rewards, but the internal satisfaction I derived from defying them by continuing to show up for classes every week was priceless.

As an added bonus, Zachary then started attending the Christian School of Ministry classes, too. Countless kids like Zachary can easily fall in with the wrong crowd when they get such outrageously long sentences for such relatively minor offenses, and all too often they end up leaving prison as much more hardened criminals than they were before, like Joseph. My hope for Zachary, though, was that he would continue taking School of Ministry classes, that he would continue to find others who would inspire him to make something better of himself, and that he would likewise inspire others to make something better of themselves.

And I'm thrilled that I got to play a small part in that, by letting Zachary see me stand up to a little religious bullying, and not allow myself to be intimidated by it. But back when I'd first met Michael at his office, I'd been seriously intimidated by the Feds' seemingly unlimited power.

CHAPTER 20

MEETING MICHAEL AT HIS OFFICE

October 30, 2009

A week after my release on bond, I was at Michael's office, with a check for the first installment of the twenty grand he'd so graciously offered to handle my federal criminal case for.

I sank into his black leather office chair and took a deep breath.

God I hope he has some good news for me. I had to borrow that five grand from my one remaining wealthy client, and if I lose my license I may never be able to afford to pay him back.

"So what are my options, Michael?" I began.

"Well, it doesn't look good. Elisa, your prosecutor, is typical for that office, unfortunately. She's young, with no real-life experience, and is looking to make a name for herself by taking down an immigration lawyer."

"What other cases has she handled?"

"Her first big success was a recent one, when she took down the Korenberg, Abramowitz and Feldun law firm for selling fake work visas. She sees your case as a mirror image of that one."

"Seriously? They couldn't be more different. Everyone knows the senior partners there always thought they were above the law. Hell, Dan Korenberg used to joke with us down at the immigration office waiting room that ethics rules didn't apply to him. Why do you think I refused to go work for them when they offered to double my salary back in the early nineties?"

"Doesn't matter, Kel. That's the frame Elisa sees your case through. Our job, then, is going to be to try to convince her that it's the wrong frame. She's got no incentive to let you off easy if she thinks you can be her next claim to fame in burnishing her reputation as the member of that office whose specialty is draining the swamp of immigration fraudsters."

"But what about that Hiram Kwan case? Didn't they accuse him of fraud, too? And wasn't he able to plead down to negligence and keep his law license?"

"Yeah, we can certainly look at his case. But our toughest sell will be trying to convince a bunch of lawyer-hating jurors that you didn't know what Joseph was up to. Most lawyers run their own offices, in their view, and so would tend to have a pretty good idea what their staff were up to."

Oh, God, I hope he doesn't think I'm an idiot for letting Joseph run the office.

"But the truth is, I didn't know. In Korenberg's case, it was their firm, and they orchestrated the fraud. In my case, it was Joseph's consulting office. I was simply 'of counsel', and he orchestrated the fraud without my either knowing about it or profiting from it."

"Who did the books?"

"Joseph."

"And did you review his numbers?"

I hung my head, gazing down at my busted shoelaces, trying to avoid his gaze. "No."

What I didn't tell him was that ever since I did the books for Pops at his Sherwin Williams Paint Store in Victoria one long ago summer, I realized two things: how much I loved hanging out with Pops, and how much I hated doing the books. Joseph loved doing the books, so I just left him to it.

"But weren't you a business major in undergrad?"

I studied my shoelaces more closely.

God, I know I'm no criminal, but why had I given Joseph enough rope to hang us both?

"Yeah, but that was just to make Mom happy. Those four years taught me a few things: that I could never be an accountant, and that more than anything else, I just wanted to be able to help people with whatever type of work I did."

"Well, it looks like, at least in the work you did with Joseph, you ended up helping everyone but yourself. Didn't you at least meet with the clients, though?"

God, I sure hope he's not already regretting having taken me on as a client.

"Only those I needed to go to interviews or court hearings with. It appears that most of the clients Joseph set up these deals with were Chinese, and so Joseph would meet with them and discuss their cases with them in Chinese when I wasn't around. He must have kept two sets of books, though, because every contract I reviewed and signed off on had the standard fees."

"Well, it sounds like we've got our work cut out for us, Kel. Here's the discovery documents," he said, handing me a pile of papers about three inches thick. "Read through them, and we'll meet again in a few weeks' time."

In that moment my greatest fear was that I might not be Lawyer Kel for much longer, and then how would I ever feel like I belonged again?

CHAPTER 21

FROM OUT OF BOUNDS TO A SERIES OF LETTERS

August-September 2013

Joseph and I both ended up doing time at the beautiful Camp Taft, in the heart of the California desert. He had arrived three and a half months before me, and, since I'd now been there for four months, and he for seven and a half, he was going to be leaving for a halfway house in another couple of weeks' time for the final two months of his ten-month sentence.

About a week had passed since the elation of my re-baptism.

On this particular day, though, I was pissed. Joseph had never been this fucking out of bounds. Except, of course, for all that immigration fraud he committed which landed us both here. But I'm just talking about our time here. Not only was he blatantly violating the rules by leaving his B Dorm home to come play Ping-Pong in my C Dorm TV room, (and nearly hitting me with the Ping- Pong ball countless times), he was running around telling everybody that would listen the lie that I had stolen seventeen grand.

Now, to begin with, if Joseph weren't so busy running the fucking commodities exchange, which involved leaving stock exchange paperwork scattered atop the Ping-Pong tables in his own dorm's TV room, he could play his fucking Ping-Pong over there, where he belongs. It was blatantly illegal, but he made no attempt to hide it. He simply had other people making the trades for him on the outside, just like he'd had the shell companies to try to hide his earlier fraud. Some people learn a few important life lessons while in prison, while people like Joseph simply learn how to be better criminals.

Thank God we never had to see each other at meals, as only one dorm at a time went to chow hall. But Joseph's prison job involved working in chow hall. And if he would have quit trying to talk to me while doing his job washing dishes in the chow hall, then I wouldn't have had to accidentally spill my fucking milk all over him earlier that morning. Anger management does have its limits, after all, and repressed rage is still rage. At least my dorm counselor was smart enough to know that there was no way in hell that I was ever gonna be willing to work in the kitchen as long as Joseph was there. But when somebody joked after the milk-spilling incident that Joseph was now looking for a lawyer, but wouldn't hire me, I joked in reply that he'd better quit looking for a free consultation from me then.

I decided to call Joseph by his Chinese name, Waiman (which is pronounced Why-Man).

"Hey, Why-Man!"

No response.

"Hey, Why-Man!!"

Joseph turned back towards the sound of my voice.

"I never stole anything!" I declared.

"I never said you stole anything," he said.

"That's not what I've been hearing around the yard."

Joseph turned and retreated hastily down the stairs.

A few minutes later, Joseph crept stealthily back into our dorm's TV room, as out of bounds as ever. I ignored him.

A gentle desert breeze wafted through my Principled Rebels' Clubhouse, in the dugout behind the baseball diamond. I couldn't help wondering what had become of Joseph's plans to become a minister. Camp Taft offers plenty of opportunities for those seeking to obtain both spiritual support and free training for the ministry.

I'd only seen Joseph attend a couple of chapel services, including once when he performed with an all-Asian choir, as Joseph is an amazing singer.

I'd never seen Joseph attend any of the dozen or more video sessions I'd been going to in the "Quest for Authentic Manhood" series. It was a series which helped us learn about ways in which our views of masculinity may have been warped by our life experiences, and how we might learn to embody a more authentic masculinity.

Nor had he ever attended any of the more than half a dozen different Chaplains College School of Ministry classes I'd been taking since my arrival four months ago.

It saddened me that Joseph's primary ministry here at Taft seemed to be, in the words of Jean Michel Basquiat, to spread the word that "those who dress better can receive Christ," just as his ministry on the outside had been.

It was a Sunday night, Joseph's last chapel service before he was gonna leave for the halfway house. While of course I was glad that he was leaving, I also wanted one last chance to pray with him, but mostly to pray for his son Justin – who is so much like me in personality – as I know this must be incredibly hard on him. Yes, I was still full of rage towards Joseph. But I didn't want his son Justin to be poisoned any further by his father's dead soul.

The day before Joseph was to be released from prison, I asked if I could write a letter to his son Justin. I'd known Joseph and his wife May and all three of their kids: Sharon the oldest, Justin in the middle, and Megan the youngest, ever since the kids, who were now in their teens, were born.

Of the three, Justin was the most like me: a deeply sensitive kid with at least one perfectionist parent. I could only imagine how his dad having been responsible for his "Uncle Kelly" being hauled off to prison must have fucked him up.

"Please do," Joseph said. "My wife and I aren't able to feel, let alone express, our emotions, and our two daughters are just like us. I'm sure he would love a letter from you."

My jaw dropped, though I tried to conceal my shock. This was the most self-aware statement I'd ever heard Joseph utter. Maybe prison had done him some good. "Great, I'll write it tonight, and give it to you tomorrow."

The letter began as follows:

"Dear Justin:

Be yourself. You are loved. God has always loved you, loves you now, and will always love you. Feel your feelings, and hopefully you won't make the same mistakes your dad and I made.

The biggest mistake I ever made was to think I had to be what everyone else wanted or needed me to be to be loved, whether it was to please my mom, to please the senior partners (other lawyers that I worked under), or to please your dad..."

Fortunately, I'd just written an angry chapter, called "Joseph's Ministry?", the night before, so I was able to write the entire ten-page letter to Justin without a single angry word about his dad. After giving Joseph the letter the next day, he said he really wanted to get together and talk before his release the next morning.

"Sure," I lied. "I'll be hanging out in my usual spot, the dugout by the baseball field." I then made sure I stayed the hell away from the dugout until it was time for our nightly lockdown. At that point I knew I would never have to see him again, as he would be locked down in a different dorm than mine until his release at dawn the next day.

* * * * *

As I thought about the letter I'd written to Justin over the next few days, it struck me that there was something odd about it. Justin and I weren't even related, and yet I was overwhelmed with concern for how fucked up he might be by this falling out between his dad and the person he thought was his dad's best friend.

Meanwhile, I had never forgiven my sister's ex-husband for having left my sister and their three kids for another woman more than twenty years before. The split had taken place right before Linda and I got married, and I'd never forgotten how my niece Melissa, our flower girl and the oldest of my sister's three kids, had thrown herself in my arms, and sobbed, "Can I come live with you two?'

I'd never been able to forgive him for abandoning the four of them, especially since my adopted sister and I both knew all too well the pain of being abandoned in early childhood.

While I could easily see how fucked-up Justin might be because of the shattered friendship between his dad and me, I was blind to how much I'd been hurting my niece and nephews by my refusal to forgive their dad. They loved their dad, and they loved their uncle, and it must have sucked for them to feel torn between the two of us.

I proceeded to write a ten-page letter to Norm, in which I apologized for having failed to forgive him for so long. My niece and nephews all expressed to me their appreciation for my finally having buried the hatchet, and, on our next trip to Abbotsford, once my probation ended, for Norm's and my nephew Thomas' graduation from my undergrad, Norm and I had a chance to further deepen our restored relationship.

* * * * *

I had written the letter to Justin as I saw him as a younger version of me.

I had written the letter to Norm as I'd seen my niece and nephews, but especially my niece Melissa, as younger versions of me.

I had written three volumes of poetry to begin excavating decades of pain which had been buried by younger versions of me.

I had begun writing this memoir as a series of letters to younger versions of me. And while that was still part of it, I had also begun to see it as a series of dialogues with my current self, asking why, for example I so desperately needed to create Kel-Dar to feel like I belonged while in prison, and letters to my future self, who would hopefully be better able to both be himself and feel like he belonged than either my younger selves or current self had managed to. Back when I'd been arrested, though, I had feared that I might never again be able to feel like I belonged, once the sexy headline of my arrest began going viral.

CHAPTER 22

THE SEXY HEADLINE

Spring 2010

I used to go to our American Immigration Lawyers' Association (AILA) monthly meetings all the time, but hadn't gone since my arrest. Then in the spring of 2010, I heard that an Assistant U.S. Attorney, from the same office that was handling my case, was going to be giving a talk. This was one meeting I simply couldn't pass up, as I wanted to hear how they approached cases like mine.

I entered the Marriott hotel conference room and sat down at a table with a half dozen of my immigration lawyer friends. The prosecutor droned on for a while as he talked about the importance of 'sending a message' by taking down lawyers who exploited their immigrant clients. Then came the line that finally helped me make sense of what had seemed at the time to be my completely unnecessary arrest at LAX a few months earlier. My friend Tom had called the lead agent to say that my lawyer was more than willing to bring me in the next morning to answer any questions they might have.

"So when we're looking to bring down an immigration lawyer," the speaker declared, "we go for the sexy headline."

As I began toying with the desserts arrayed in front of me, the absence of fact-checking in both the Department of Homeland Security's press release and all the news articles which followed began to make perfect sense. For they knew all along that it was Joseph's office, and I was simply 'of counsel' to him, and that only Joseph and his wife had invested their illegally obtained funds in funeral plots. Since the Feds knew all this, only Joseph and his wife were ever charged with money laundering. The articles, however, rewrote the script by pretending that I was the 'owner' of the firm, and Joseph and his wife simply my 'business associates,' and then kept the fantasy going by pretending that all three of us had 'laundered the profits by buying vacant burial plots.' I finally settled on the blueberry pie, since it had the same first letters as 'burial plots.'

I had to hand it to them. *Lawyer arrested for selling fake work visas* was a way sexier headline than *Lawyer surrenders voluntarily to answer questions about actions he knew nothing about and made no money from.*

CHAPTER 23

THE DEATH AND REBIRTH OF HOPE

September 2013

Hope is a fragile enough commodity at the best of times. In prison, hope, which seemed solid as a rock one moment, could sink like quicksand the next.

I was beginning to feel like I'd made it over some massive hurdles.

And then I slammed headfirst into a wall. Linda had called a couple of days earlier and said that she'd received a letter from a law firm stating that they'd obtained a default judgement against me for a Citibank Master Card account I'd once had for thirty-four grand. When she'd first mentioned it, I'd thought it was a simple matter of identity theft, and asked her to let our upstairs neighbor, who's a lawyer himself, take care of it for me.

But then I thought about it some more. After my initial arrest back in the fall of 2009, I'd doubled down on my efforts to try to save the handful of immigrant clients I had left. Thing is, however, I'm a terrible businessman. So as the debts of all my overhead expenses continued to pile up, and my revenues continued to dwindle, I proceeded to max out every credit card I had.

Finally, however, having relocated my office several times, I was forced to let the last of my staff go, and try to figure out a way to settle my debts without declaring bankruptcy.

After every bank I attempted to settle my debts with directly refused to do so, I finally hired a firm named Legal Helpers to negotiate my debt settlements on my behalf. Unfortunately, though, midway through those negotiations, Legal Helpers relocated from the west coast to the Midwest, and my account apparently failed to get the attention it deserved.

Legal Helpers assured me, however, that most of my debts had been settled prior to their office relocation. And when I finally managed to obtain a settlement in a personal injury case after I suffered severe nerve damage and reflex sympathetic dystrophy in a car accident, I was able to pay off every outstanding unsettled account that I was aware of, thus narrowly avoiding debtor's prison.

Unfortunately, however, it seems the Citibank debt had fallen through the cracks. It was not on the list of unsettled accounts I received from Legal Helpers. Nor had any of its lawyers' letters managed to reach me at my most recent Post Office Box mailing address, as apparently mail sent to Post Office Boxes cannot be forwarded.

If my six grand fine had been a daunting task for me – with nothing to my name – to envision paying off, a forty grand debt was an impossibility. The hope that I had worked so hard to sustain was fading fast.

Later that evening, I ran into the surprisingly human Pastor Marvin, one of the prison's Christian School of Ministry pastors. When I'd been suspended and removed from the School of Ministry for changing my religion to Native American, I'd initially been so blinded by frustration at being denied the right to obtain my free associate degree in theology over this that I couldn't see the big picture.

Pastor Marvin, by contrast, was far better able to see the whole of the moon. He said that if two applicants came to him seeking to be ministers in his church, one with an associate degree in theology and the other with a deep passion for relational ministry, he'd look at each of them and see how best they could serve the church, not which one of them happened to have the degree. This reminded me of how Joseph and I used to view those seeking to work in our office so differently, as Joseph had prioritized book smarts, while I had emphasized the importance of relational skills.

This conversation with Pastor Marvin had greatly encouraged me. He had told me how badly he felt about the way the School of Ministry had treated me, and that he wished he were in a position with sufficient authority to be able to convince them to reverse their position. He said that the unforgivable sin is clearly not changing one's religion to Native American, but rather having an unforgiving spirit. And I knew that I needed healing from my own unforgiving spirit, towards Joseph, towards my prosecutor, and towards many others, as much as the School of Ministry chaplains might need healing from theirs. For some time after my arrest, however, I'd been unaware of just how deep my need for psychological and spiritual healing was. I just knew I needed help.

CHAPTER 24

PSYCHOLOGICAL HEALING, PART 1

Spring 2011-Fall 2011

After learning about how cases like mine were tried, I started wondering why I'd believed Joseph so much that I'd given him enough rope to hang us both. Had it had something to do with my childhood? And if so, what?

And then, as if by kismet, one day in the spring of 2011, as I was out for a drive in Santa Monica, an episode of *This American Life* began playing on KCRW. The program was about attachment disorder, something I'd never heard of. I was fascinated by the program, however, as they were talking about a group of adoptees who, despite having been adopted by loving families, tended to act out in frequently self-destructive ways, which understandably deeply troubled and mystified their adoptive families.

They had finally been diagnosed with attachment disorder, which is a condition that stems from a lack of basic trust that anyone was truly going to be there for them. This lack of basic trust had sprung from their having been abruptly separated from their primary caregiver, usually either their birthmother or foster mother, between the ages of six months and three years. While most of the time they would consciously strive to do everything they could to prove that they were worthy of being loved, when they acted out, they would unconsciously strive to do all they could to prove that they were unworthy of being loved. Their behavior mirrored mine much too closely for comfort, while my abrupt separation from my foster mom Grace when I was eleven months old echoed their early childhood separation experiences also.

I found myself drawn in by their stories, as just like those kids doing everything they could to prove themselves worthy of love, I remembered how I had spent most of my life first trying to excel in school and desperately trying to prove myself worthy of my adoptive mom's love, and later trying to succeed in being, and being seen as, a deeply compassionate immigration lawyer, desperately trying to prove myself worthy of my immigrant clients' and Joseph's love.

But then, these very same kids would act out in ways which seemed determined to demonstrate that they were unworthy of being loved. I had done that. I'd crashed and burned in my first semester of my first year of law school, seemingly subconsciously destroying in a single semester the myth of the brilliant scholar I'd fought so hard to sustain for so long. My arrest at LAX had similarly seemingly subconsciously destroyed in a single moment the role of the deeply caring immigration lawyer I'd fought so hard to play for so long.

"My God, those kids sound just like me!" I exclaimed aloud in the car, to no one in particular.

Because I was adopted I would either try to belong by playing whatever role my caregivers demanded of me, like being "Smart Kel" or "Martyr Kel" so that I would feel like I belonged to my adoptive mom, or I would tend to excessively trust those, like Joseph, who seemed like insiders who could help even an outsider like me feel like he belonged.

As the episode went on to explain, since adoptees are often convinced that they will eventually be abandoned no matter what they do, they tend to act out in hurtful ways, which then serves to drive those who care about them away. This then allows the adoptee to say, "See, I knew I would be abandoned."

The episode went on to describe one of the therapies for this disorder, which was called "Love or Die." Hearing this gave me chills.

My case, meanwhile, had now dragged on for about a year and a half, and it had become painfully obvious that the prosecutor held all the cards, and so there was no need for her to even pretend to negotiate. Something about this episode on attachment disorder, however, had revived a nagging feeling I'd had ever since my case began, that there had to be a psychological component to my having trusted Joseph so much.

By the fall of 2011, with my case now nearing the two-year mark, I was already pretty sure that I was suffering from attachment disorder, and that this had somehow played a role in my relationship with Joseph. I had excessively trusted him because he seemed like an insider who could help even an outsider like me feel like he belonged, and then I'd subconsciously allowed him to abuse my trust to the point where he could destroy us both. In my desperation to not be abandoned by him, I had abandoned myself. I had avoided therapy my whole life, naively believing that I could write my way through any trauma life threw at me, but this one was way more than I could handle.

Somehow, I felt, my trusting Joseph had to be related to my being adopted, had to be related to my struggles with attachment disorder, had to be related to my having lost my adoptive dad to that permanent head injury from a near-fatal car crash when I was halfway around the world in London for my first semester of my last year of law school. But how were all these things connected? And could they be used in my defense?

My lawyer, Michael A., had resisted my requests to go that route, however, as he told me that judges and juries alike tended to be extremely skeptical when it came to psychological evidence. However, after two years of battering himself bloody against a brick wall of a prosecutor for whom stonewalling our every attempt to negotiate seemed to be second nature, he finally relented.

"Okay," he finally said, "Go ahead and try to find a forensic psychologist and see if they might be willing to prepare an expert report concerning the psychological aspects of your case. We'll see if it might help us or not." In other words, if the expert report was able to show how I was psychologically pre-disposed to trust Joseph more than some other lawyer might have, perhaps this would help the prosecutor see my case through new eyes. Since the prosecutor seemed to be convinced that I was the orchestrator of this fraud, if this report could help her see that Joseph had orchestrated it, and that I had naively trusted him far more than I should have, and in so doing had subconsciously allowed him to abuse my trust in order to get away with his fraud, she might then be willing to negotiate with us at long last.

Having worked with several different clinical psychologists who'd helped prepare expert reports for my immigrant clients over the years,

I reached out to see if they might be able to refer me to somebody who might be able to help me with my case.

One of them recommended a forensic psychologist named Michael P. down in Orange County, whose areas of expertise included attachment disorder. I called his office, scheduled an initial consultation, and drove down to meet him for the first time.

After a few nervous minutes checking out the magazines and celebrity endorsements in his waiting area, he ushered me in and proceeded to ask me several questions about my case. Near the end of my initial intake interview, I asked him, "So do you think you might be able to help me out with my case?"

"Sure, for ten thousand dollars," he replied with a perfectly straight face.

"Are you kidding me? My lawyer's only charging me twenty grand, and he's been fighting for me for over two years now! Why is your help going to cost me half that?"

"Because my rate is three hundred dollars an hour. You will need to come in for several additional intake interviews, and take half a dozen different psychological tests. I will then need to analyze the results of both your interviews and all those tests and prepare a detailed report for the court. That will require at least thirty-five to forty hours of my time, so you're getting a better deal by my giving you a flat rate of only ten grand."

Despite my sticker shock at what I felt was his taking advantage of a vulnerable client, at this point I was desperately seeking any potential "silver bullet" for my case, which seemed to have fallen into a black hole.

"All right, if that's the lowest rate you can give me. Can I at least pay it in two or three monthly installments?"

"Sure, I'll put that in the contract."

I returned about a week later, having borrowed the first installment from my lone remaining wealthy immigrant client. Since my criminal case had not yet been decided, I was still able to represent a handful of clients who had not abandoned ship, as well as do contract work for other lawyers.

As promised, he gave me about a half dozen psychological tests to take, and for the next several hours I did my best to answer all the questions as truthfully as I could. The tests were wide-ranging, but revolved around trying to determine what my state of mind was, and what my psychological profile might be. But once another week had passed, he called me back and said, "I'm afraid you're going to have to retake those tests I gave you last week. Your results indicate that you are in the two percent of the population so traumatized that there's no psychological category for you. Without a category, I can't possibly prepare a report for you."

"Seriously, the top two percent? My mom will be so proud!" I joked. But the truth was, I was oddly proud, even though this was not the sort of test I should have taken any pleasure or pride in having scored in the top two percent on. It seemed I had so absorbed the frame of being a victim, from the shock of having had my trust abused by Joseph, my friend of twenty years, coupled with the stress of having been subjected to the abusiveness of the criminal justice system for the past couple of years, that I could no longer see myself outside the prison walls of that frame of shame. Yet in some weird way, that "frame of shame" felt like a badge of honor to me.

I took the long, slow drive down to Yorba Linda, home of the Richard Nixon library, and felt a strange kinship with that embattled former president as I made my way back to the psychologist's office to retake the tests. As I was driving, I left about a dozen desperate messages with friends, hoping against hope that at least one of them might be able to help me wrap my head around this latest bombshell. Moments before I reached my destination, my spiritual mentor John Tiersma Watson returned my call. Upon hearing my description of my non-diagnosis diagnosis, he calmly replied, "That's wonderful news. It means you're not sufficiently socialized for conformity."

Because of his words, I confidently re-took those tests. Even though that second round of tests did confirm that I was suffering from both attachment disorder and post-traumatic stress disorder, I was relieved NOT to have finished in the top two percent this time, and to be rid of that weird sick pride at having been so well-defined by my sense of victimhood. Finally, my lifelong addiction to chaos and recurring struggles with acting out behaviors had an explanatory diagnosis, and my healing journey, no matter how circuitous, could finally begin. Thanks to John's encouragement, I felt a greater sense of agency this time, in that my nonconformity was not so much an involuntary response to trauma but rather a deliberate choice to do what I felt needed to be done.

CHAPTER 25

FROM LEGALISTIC, ARROGANT, WEALTHY LONER, ABDICATOR AND WIMP TO EMPATHETIC, PATIENT KING, WARRIOR, LOVER AND FRIEND

October 2013

I had learned a lot of painful lessons from my "Quest for Authentic Manhood" class earlier this evening. To begin with, I'd begun the class thinking that I'd somehow managed to avoid succumbing to the three reasons many lawyers became so miserable: they either became legalistic, arrogant, and/or addicted to the wealth that could often become their primary purpose for remaining in a profession they'd long since lost the heart for. I thought to myself, no, that couldn't possibly be me, I'm not like all those other lawyers. Mom was incredibly legalistic, with her repeated insistence that my "will must be broken," a reflection of her belief that I was incapable of following the rules, as in her world, only those who follow the rules (aka: legalists) could be saved.

But then it hit me. I'd been far too much like those other lawyers, but had just been too blind to see it. Hell yeah, I was legalistic. I figured if I just followed the rules, like Mom's about needing to sacrifice myself, and martyred myself on behalf of my clients, and, eventually, on behalf of Joseph, that I'd somehow earn the right to not be abandoned. When Joseph then abandoned me, however, my sense of entitlement got ripped right out from under me.

And hell yeah, I was arrogant. I thought if I could somehow save my immigrant clients, and eventually Joseph, that I'd be just fine. I was blind to the fact that I was as much in need of saving as Joseph or any of my clients.

And hell yeah, I was moderately wealthy. Not as defined by the Josephs of the world, of course, with their mansions worth a million and a half. But my sixty-thousand-dollar annual income would be considered wealthy by worldwide standards, as it made me part of the "1%" I so loved to throw stones at here within the U.S. Even within the U.S., however, it would have put me within the top ten percent. So, compared to most other lawyers, I was a starving lawyer. As my namesake Einstein would say, "It's all relative." Yes, the pre-trial services officer at my bond hearing had been shocked at how little I'd made. However, relative to how little most Americans make, I was at least relatively wealthy. And long after my passion for my profession had died, the fact that I could still make that sixty grand a year kept me going into the office, day after soul-sucking day.

But in the authentic manhood class tonight I also learned that the "four faces" of a balanced man are those of a king, warrior, lover, and friend. A king was a leader, a warrior was a fighter, and a friend was someone willing to hold their friends accountable. And I was a most unbalanced man, it seemed, as I had only fully embraced and developed the face of the lover. As to the other three, rather than my being a friend, king, or warrior, I had become a Loner, Abdicator, and a Wimp, the first letters of which, just like the Legalistic, Arrogant, Wealth-seeker I refused to acknowledge I was, spelt LAW.

And these three labels really hit home. For when it came to the qualities of a friend, especially in my relationship with Joseph, I'd been excessively loyal and trusting, and insufficiently challenging of Joseph to hold him either transparent or accountable. This had enabled Joseph to conduct his fraud without my knowledge. I was way too much of a loner to be able to challenge or hold Joseph accountable for his conduct. I was also way too much of a loner to have anyone in my life I could be transparent enough with for them to be able to hold me accountable for the way my heart was no longer in my work.

And when it came to the qualities of a king, such as nobility, integrity, and strong convictions, those didn't count for shit when it came to my relationship with Joseph. It seems I lacked the courage of my convictions, and so abdicated my rightful leadership role which my position as lawyer should have led me to.

But it was with the qualities of a warrior where my failures really burned brightest. Who cares that my name, Kelly, means "brave warrior"? Who cares that my Scots-Irish bloodline is full of people who James Webb describes as having been "born fighting"? The bottom line for me was that I hated conflict. So yeah, when necessary, I fought like hell for my clients, and fought like hell when I thought Joseph was being falsely accused of fraud. But initiating conflict scared the shit out of me, especially with people like Joseph who provided me with a deep sense of safety and security. The one fight I needed to have, with Joseph, to protect, shield, and defend myself, I was way too afraid to have.

I could now see I had my work cut out for me. I'd need to work like hell to be transparent enough in my relationships with others so I can do a much better job of weeding out false friendships and cultivating true friendships of mutual accountability. I'd need to learn to courageously embrace my inner leader, the one I never dared to imagine myself being. And lastly, I'd need to learn to fight like hell to better protect, shield and defend myself, as fighting for everybody but myself hadn't exactly worked out too well for me.

On October 15th, about a week after that "Quest for Authentic Manhood" class, where I'd gained so much insight into who I'd been as a lawyer, I'd dutifully shown up at the prison's medical office to see the doctor to get my convalescence extended, as I had not yet had an MRI for my Achilles injury four and a half months earlier. After waiting around for nearly two hours, the female nurse we'd nicknamed Hic-Bot simply said, "Come back at 3. Where was it you worked before?"

"The Native American Garden."

So much for seeing the doctor.

A few minutes later, at around 8:45 in the morning, now back for a short nap in my cell, the female guard we'd nicknamed Fem-Bot screamed at us, "Ok, everybody up! You should have your beds made up by 9 am!"

Fortunately, I was taking a nap on my "permanently made" bed, so I continued my nap.

A few minutes later, however, over the public address system came the following announcement: "Keely Geelez, report immediately to Camp Control."

I then wearily trudged over to Camp Control, where a male officer, who we'd nicknamed Officer Bare-Ass (I think his actual name was Barry, but we preferred nicknames for all the robots in this place), who was in charge of all the outdoor work assignments, including the Native American Garden, yelled at me, "Why'd you tell the nurse just now that you worked in the Native American Garden before?"

"Because that's where I worked. They're under your jurisdiction, right?"

"You work where I tell you to work. Nobody works in the Native American Garden. They're all volunteers. I'm just kind enough to let them get paid."

"Ok, good to know. Thanks."

A few hours later, I returned to the medical office for the noon pill call to pick up my Neurontin. This time it was the female nurse we'd nicknamed Bro-Bot who interrogated me. "So did you figure out where you used to work yet?"

"You mean, did you guys figure it out?"

"That's it. I'm calling Security. Just wait outside. Officer Burns wants to see you." (Robots still called each other by name, as they were trying to pass for human. We simply called him Officer Burn-Ass).

While waiting outside Medical, I saw Officer Burn-Ass leave the medical office and head over to Camp Control. A few minutes later, I saw Officer Burn-Ass leave Camp Control and I went up to him.

"Did you need to see me for anything? As I'm running late for my 12:30 screenwriting class."

"Who are you?"

"Never mind, I thought maybe you needed to see me for some reason. My mistake."

I then went back inside the medical office, where I saw Nurse Hic-Bot.

"I need my ID card back so I can get to my screenwriting class."

"Don't you want to know what's happening with your convalescence extension request?"

"If I can get an answer soon. I'm already late for my class."

"It'll be at least fifteen minutes. Come back after your class. Here's your ID card."

"Thanks."

I then headed off to my screenwriting class. After class, I returned to the medical center, where Nurse Hic-Bot and Nurse Bro-Bot immediately called Officer Bare-Ass over.

Nurse Hic-Bot then told me "We're denying your convalescence extension request."

"But where's the orthopedic doctor? I was supposed to see him about my request."

"He's not here."

Nurse Bro-Bot then chimed in: "Plus, you smirk too much to be granted a convalescence extension."

"Ok, great, now I've heard everything."

Officer Bare-Ass then added, "So you either start cleaning windows for me tomorrow morning at 6:30, or we can send you across the street." (All of us inmates knew what "across the street" meant: it meant that we were being banished to the SHU, or "Special Housing Unit", aka the hole, aka solitary confinement.)

"But I still haven't gotten my MRI, which the orthopedic doctor said I needed. And my wife, who works in a hospital, said that it would be absurd for you to try to put me back to work without an MRI. But if you say I gotta be there at 6:30 tomorrow morning, I'll be there at 6:30 tomorrow morning."

Here's what it came down to. A morning compound supervisor, Officer Bare-Ass, and two female nurses, Officers Hic-Bot and Bro-Bot, had decided to try to intimidate me into risking permanent damage to my right Achilles by denying my convalescence extension request. By doing so they had defied three doctors – two prison doctors and one outside orthopedic doctor – all of whom had ordered MRIs for me.

This sounded like a great opportunity to see if I was willing to take my own advice and not let them intimidate me. We'd soon find out, as six thirty the next morning was coming soon.

The next day, it suddenly dawned on me that one of two scenarios had played out in the medical office yesterday. In one, the most bizarre imaginable, the prison doctor we'd nicknamed Doc-Hol had taken leave of his senses. That same prison doctor, just two and a half weeks earlier, had renewed his order for an MRI for my right Achilles and extended my convalescent status. Had he now suddenly ordered my convalescence status terminated, despite my still not having gotten my MRI? Had he forgotten about the life-threatening right leg infection I'd told him about that I'd been hospitalized for just two years earlier? Was he going to be as careless about his physician's license as the prosecutor believed I had been with my law license?

The other, far more plausible scenario, was that three non-doctors, Nurses Hic-Bot and Bro-Bot and Officer Bare-Ass, had risked Doc-Hol's physician's license without his knowledge. They had done so by denying my convalescence extension request, and threatening to send me to the SHU if I refused to show up for work the next day in the morning compound at 630 am.

This far more likely scenario helped me better understand how I'd ended up losing my law license. A handful of my immigrant clients had been fooled into believing that my non-lawyer friend and colleague Joseph (who would later become my co-defendant) knew the law better than I did, so there was no need to check with me to see if what he was doing was legal. For immigrants, just like inmates, can be very easily frightened, and since they have so few rights, they feel powerless. This makes them easy targets for manipulation, intimidation, and/or abuse.

When I showed up the next day at 6:30 am in the morning compound to report for duty, I asked Officer Bare-Ass, "How badly do you want this lawsuit?"

"Your convalescence extension request has been granted. You may go now."

I couldn't help but smirk as I made my way back to my dorm.

I'd never have gotten to the place of being able to stand up to this level of bullying, however, had I not begun by acknowledging my need for both spiritual and psychological healing in the aftermath of my arrest and during my time under indictment.

CHAPTER 26

SPIRITUAL HEALING

Winter 2011

Now that I had a diagnosis, I was looking for what might help heal it, and I thought that might be prayer. For the decade I'd been working with Joseph, I'd taken my faith for granted, and rarely attended church. Just as there are no atheists in foxholes, there are none in prison or under indictment. Ever since I'd been under indictment, I'd been attending church every Sunday, and going up for after-service prayer every Sunday. I sensed that my healing would require not just psychological, but also spiritual, help.

The Sunday after I received my diagnosis, I was feeling cursed. Curses to me have always felt very person- and geography-specific. My relationship with Joseph, from Hong Kong, felt cursed. Likewise, my relationship with my Grampa Bob, from Northern Ireland, felt cursed.

That Sunday, a missionary couple, Mark and Darlene Harper, came back from Hong Kong to visit our church. Mark's sermon struck a chord with me. What really hit home, though, was when Darlene said, in the call to prayer, that she sensed that one or more of us were feeling like we had "laid everything at the altar, and God had been silent." I went up for prayer, summarized for Mark what the past couple of years since my arrest had been like, and he prayed with me.

The next Sunday after church, Mark asked me for an update, and I shared with him briefly.

Darlene then asked me a few questions, and I summarized for her what the past two years had been like for me.

"You must feel cursed," she replied.

"Hell, yeah."

God, it felt good to be seen so clearly.

The very next Sunday, I was so desperate for prayer, I stuck around after church for an extra three hours for the next intensive prayer training session, as I knew I'd at least be able to get some small group prayer during the final half hour. Once the prayer session ended, I asked the group leader if he had any suggestions as to where I might be able to find more prayer support.

He encouraged me to come out that Tuesday evening for a special summer school class featuring Jean Darnall. Eighty-eight years of age but still going strong, Darnall was known for having a powerful prophetic prayer ministry.

When I showed up on Tuesday and offered them one of my poetry books to get in (as classes cost $15), they politely declined, but realizing my abject poverty, offered me a scholarship instead. At one point during her talk, when Jean Darnall shared that she sensed that one or more of us who were there that night felt like a "stranded servant", I knew I was where I was meant to be. I then asked her during a break where I might get more prayer, and she said she led prayer services on Thursdays at noon at Church on the Way in Van Nuys. When she prayed over me at the end of the session, she said that she sensed that I was "full of the spirit, and just waiting for it to be released."

Given how few clients I had left at that time, I made the hour long drive up to Van Nuys the following Thursday, then spent another three hours at this prayer service, once again getting small group prayer. Now my maternal Irish grandpa Bob, with whom I felt my "curse of buried feelings" had begun, had grown up in Belfast, Northern Ireland, in County Armagh. Now of all the people in the world for me to meet, there was a pastoral couple from County Armagh who Jean Darnall had shared a prophetic word with some four decades earlier, who had been led by God to come thank her personally that day. While we were waiting in line for prayer, the wife of that couple told me that she had been given a word from the Lord for me, which was found in Proverbs 26:2, that "an undeserved curse shall not alight."

Now that my spiritual healing journey had begun, I was reminded that I had once thought I didn't need any spiritual healing at all, as I'd been working with a guy I thought could be spiritual enough for the both of us.

CHAPTER 27

FROM WHAT IS PRAYER
TO DIVING INTO DARKNESS

October 2013

I'd just gotten back to my dorm from my Christian School of Ministry class and was reflecting on the homework assignment, which was to ask ourselves the question "What is Prayer?", when I came up with the following answer.

Prayer is stripping ourselves naked before God, and then waiting, waiting, patiently waiting for God to clothe us. The hardest thing by far about prayer is the waiting for God to clothe us, as my natural human tendency is to spend most of my time in prayer telling God what I wanna wear, and quickly forgetting that it was my terrible wardrobe choices that drove me to prayer in the first place. For as long as I cling to the illusion that I can clothe myself, God cannot clothe me.

I need prayer to remind me how utterly naked I must be in God's presence, and how my foolish attempts to clothe myself have driven me away from God's unconditional love.

I felt like I'd been reborn. A few days after I'd discovered the true meaning of prayer, I'd read Jonathan Franzen's essay entitled "Why Bother", from his essay collection *How to be Alone*, and when he wrote about living in a country which felt "hopelessly unmoored from reality," it had helped crystallize much of the despair I'd been feeling since my arrest at LAX four years earlier. Reading had been my lifeline throughout my life, and reading essays like this one reminded me of how reading had always helped me feel less alone.

Later that evening, I was outside in my Principled Rebels' Clubhouse, gazing at the moon.

Now, instead of the invisible prison of frozen feelings I'd been trapped in before, I was in an actual fucking prison. Ironically, I'd never felt freer in my life. I was finally free to dive into the darkness of my soul, and into the darkness of others' souls. I'd finally begun to realize that I wouldn't drown there. But there'd been a point while I was under indictment when I truly feared that I might drown in the darkness.

CHAPTER 28

BREAST CANCER BREAKING POINT

Winter 2011

By the winter of 2011, the prosecutor was still refusing to negotiate, while Michael P., the forensic psychiatrist I'd hired, was still refusing to finish preparing his expert report for me, as I had been unable to come up with his final installment payment yet. When I finally managed to make the payment, he put the finishing touches on his report, which I then showed to Michael A. to see if we might be able to use it.

A few days later, I called Michael A. to see what he thought of the report.

"I'm sorry, but there's no way in hell we can submit this report. It makes you sound so crazy that you should probably have never been a lawyer in the first place."

"In other words, it sounds like it's close to the truth. But you're right, not so helpful for my case."

Wow, what a waste of ten grand that was, I thought to myself. It seemed that instead of a "silver bullet", I'd accidentally purchased a poison pill.

And then things got worse.

My wife Linda came back from her oncologist with the following news. "The biopsy on my left breast indicated invasive cancer," she said, her voice quivering.

"No! It's been seven years since you last had it. You've been eating healthy and working out. I've been green juicing for you. How could it possibly have come back?"

"It's the stress of your case, dear. I'm an empath, and no matter how hard I tried to shield myself from your pain, my body couldn't."

Her breast cancer surgery was scheduled for a Monday in late January of 2012. As luck would have it, my prosecutor had given me a "drop-dead date" of Tuesday, the day after Linda's surgery, to respond to her latest non-offer on my case.

Linda's breast cancer surgeon this time around just happened to be Middle Eastern, and so when we told her about my case's drop-dead date, and that it was the Department of Homeland Security that had brought the case against me, she immediately offered to write a letter to both the judge and prosecutor for me. "I get racially profiled at LAX all the time," this sweet, world-renowned breast cancer surgeon said.

The prosecutor was clearly moved by my wife's surgeon's letter. She offered me a two- day extension of my drop-dead date, which would now fall on the Thursday of the week of my wife's surgery. Then, shortly after completing Linda's surgery, her surgeon came out with a look of grave concern on her face.

"One of Linda's lymph nodes does not look good," she said.

There was no way I was going to tell Linda that. So that whole week, I wandered around in a daze. I wept. I feared the worst. What if it's metastasized? She may die. I can't live without her. Why the fuck is all of this happening, God?

Responding to the prosecutor's arbitrary drop-dead date for her bullshit plea was the least of my concerns. I was in no fucking emotional state to do so.

Thank God the judge had been sufficiently moved by Linda's surgeon's letter to grant us a few months' extension in which to respond.

And thank God that on Friday, the day after the prosecutor's drop-dead date, Linda's surgeon informed us that Linda's cancer had been invasive and would require further treatment, but had not, in fact, metastasized to the lymph nodes.

But now I knew that it was no longer a question of if, but when, my old life as a lawyer was going to end.

CHAPTER 29

63 DAYS TILL SEMI-FREEDOM

October 2013

Red and I were in the same dorm, and Red had invited me to do some laps of the track with him. As we walked around the track, I learned that we shared a passion for justice and, in the absence of justice, for dark comedy.

"How'd you end up in here?" I asked him.

"I did some tax preparation work for some clients, who then, without my knowledge, committed fraud. The feds charged me with conspiracy," Red replied, wiping the sweat from his brow as he quickened his pace.

"Sounds painfully familiar. Did you take a plea?"

"Hell, no. They threatened to double my sentence if I went to trial, but I didn't care. I went to trial, and, despite my having clearly established that I knew nothing about the fraud, they said that because I had prepared the tax forms that were later used to commit the fraud and the fraud could not have been committed without my forms, I was therefore guilty of conspiracy. And, just as they'd threatened, they doubled my sentence from three years to six."

"Damn, they threatened me with a possible six-year sentence if I dared take them to trial too. Now it seems I really dodged a bullet by taking a plea. That must really piss you off though, eh?"

"Sometimes, yeah. But most of the time I'm too busy fighting like hell for my fellow inmates here at Taft. So far I've drafted legal briefs for over twenty of them, and managed to get reduced sentences for a dozen."

"But I thought you were a tax accountant on the outside?" I said, adjusting my tattered white baseball cap to keep from being blinded by the sun.

"I was. But having to fight my own case meant I had to learn a hell of a lot of criminal law, so even if that knowledge couldn't save me, at least I'm putting it to good use by helping others get released sooner."

"Wow. You're an amazing jailhouse lawyer, especially for not having even been a lawyer on the outside." I, by contrast, no longer had the stomach to spend any time doing legal research for myself (as it was too late) or for anyone else, as I had been left far too embittered by the brutal end of my own case.

"Thanks man. Now let's finish this damn lap and get out of the sun. I'm a redhead, and me and the sun don't get along real well together."

"Sounds good."

Around three weeks after Red and I had that conversation on the track, I had turned fifty. To celebrate the occasion, Red had encouraged me to write up the guard who'd deprived me of breakfast that morning because I'd forgotten to remove my baseball cap.

Five months later, I realized that I was going to miss Red when he left the next day. I just hoped I could learn to fight for myself the way that Red has fought for both me and countless others during his time here at Taft.

"The spirit of Red is within me," I assured myself.

Red had given me the best farewell gift. After six months of sleeping on a metal bunkbed with a wafer-thin mattress, Red had graciously gifted me with his "prison-pedic" mattress, which meant that I could finally no longer feel the metal bunkbed beneath me. I had slept like a baby for the first time in months. I now wanted to carry on Red's spirit during my final two months here, by standing up to and exposing abusers of power as he had done, and so hopefully helping spare others the hell of abuse by doing so.

At my first meal since Red's departure, I was heartened at being joined at lunch by my fellow reader and dormmate Rod. Thanks to Rod's generosity, I'd been able to surround my chow hall mystery meat hockey puck like substance with real tomatoes, bell peppers, onions, and mustard. All that was missing was the avocado and barbecue sauce, of which there simply wasn't enough to spare. By doing so, Rod had managed to make my meal, quite miraculously, enjoyable. But long before Red and Rod had helped with my psychological healing while in prison, I'd finally figured out that I needed to begin that healing journey while I'd been under indictment.

CHAPTER 30

PSYCHOLOGICAL HEALING, PART 2

Spring 2012-Fall 2012

I clearly needed to start seeing a therapist. I'd managed to avoid doing so my entire life, even when I had suffered a near-nervous breakdown and succumbed to an addiction of three to four sleeping pills a night in response to my insomnia from having blown my scholarship during my first semester at Pepperdine Law School. I just figured I could write my way through any trauma, and throughout that insane semester, I started a memoir with a working title of *Roadmaps through Hell.* God, how prophetic that turned out to be!

Yet had I gone to see a therapist after Pops had suffered that traumatic brain injury after his near-fatal car crash during my first semester of my last year of law school in the fall of 1988, maybe my post-traumatic stress disorder would have been diagnosed a quarter century earlier than it finally was.

Maybe I would have realized that I needed saving as much as any of my immigrant clients did.

Maybe I would have realized that I was drawn to working with Joseph because I was longing for a father.

But when the bottom had fallen out of my life with my arrest at LAX, it had become painfully obvious to me that my life-long avoidance of therapy had been a major fuck-up. It seems I had to get arrested and spend three and a half years fighting to keep my law license and stay out of prison before I was forced to face the fact that I must have had some deep unhealed psychological wounds.

There was no way in hell I could afford Michael P. at three hundred dollars an hour. Fortunately, however, he had informed me that there were graduate school psychology programs and non-profits that offered sliding scale therapy services, ideal for starving federally indicted lawyers like me.

Having gone to Pepperdine for law school, I began my low-cost therapy adventures with Pepperdine's graduate school psychology program. And while I felt the therapist who tried to help me there was able to be a decent "mirror" to help me better understand my trauma, the depth of my trauma seemed overwhelming to her, making it much harder for her to really be much of a "ladder" for me in terms of suggestions on ways to begin healing from it. After a few months of sessions with her, however, I had to wrestle with my abandonment fears once again, as she informed me that she would soon be graduating from the program, and so it was time for me to try to find a new therapist.

I next tried to find a therapist through the Airport Marina Counseling Center. However, they were booked solid, and so they put me on their waiting list. Anxious to not be kept waiting too long between therapists, I booked a session with a therapist at the Maple Counseling Center.

Unlike the Pepperdine therapist, however, who I at least felt got me even if she could not do much to help me, during my first session with the Maple Center therapist I felt more like I was being preached at than really listened to.

Fortunately, though, I didn't have to be preached at any longer than that single session, for before my next scheduled session at Maple I received a call back from Airport Marina saying that they had found a therapist for me.

As soon as I entered Jody's small office at the Airport Marina Counseling Center, I felt like I'd finally come home. After I shared a brief summary of the hell I'd been going through for the past three years, his first words to me were, "We're going to be doing a lot of soul work in here." I exhaled softly. After my earlier experiences with a mercenary therapist, an overwhelmed therapist, and a condescending therapist, I now knew that I'd finally found the right therapist to accompany me on this soul-work I was so clearly in need of. Had I known at the time that soul work amounts to a long descent into unforgiving darkness, until you find the song that sings you home, I might not have been quite so eager to begin. But it was heal or die time now.

CHAPTER 31

SUSPENDED, REMOVED AND UNREGISTERED

October 24, 2013

It was late October of 2013. A few days after Red's departure, I was amused by the fact that when I showed up for my Christian School of Ministry classes that night, not only had I been suspended and removed, but I'd now been "unregistered" as well. Good thing I snagged a copy of the course materials before they tried to steal those away from me too. Note to self: Be sure to grab the course materials as soon I arrive for my leadership class this coming Sunday before they try to deny me those too.

The absurdity level just kept right on rising throughout the first session, as the same chaplain, Cha-Cha-Sca, who'd suspended and removed (and now, apparently, unregistered) me, tried to impress us with the toughness of his new regime. He threatened to deduct ten percent off our grade for each class we showed up more than five minutes late for. It's a good thing I'd already been suspended and removed, then. I could go ahead and show up more than five minutes late for all ten classes (like I would have anyways), then ace all my weekly homework assignments, ace my final paper and final exam, and end up with the same grade of O as somebody who hadn't been suspended and removed, but simply showed up late for all ten classes, despite acing everything else. The other slightly less robotic chaplain, Cha-Hoorah, had at least had the good sense to set a maximum penalty for tardiness and/or absenteeism at five percent total for the entire ten-week session.

For a moment, however, we all thought Cha-Cha-Sca had come to his senses. He actually reduced the first weekly assignment from two six-to-nine hundred word essays, one on First Peter and the other on Second

Peter, to a single six hundred to nine hundred word essay on both. But he then immediately returned to Absurdistan by insisting on three separate six hundred to nine hundred word essays on First, Second and Third John. Okay, First John has four chapters, no problem there. But Second and Third John have thirteen and fourteen verses, respectively. I couldn't wait to see what literary masterpiece I could come up with for those two, now that I was expected to write at least fifty to sixty words for each fucking verse! Good thing I didn't have any grades to worry about, so I could just let her rip.

Early the next morning, from my perch in the Clubhouse, I could see that the first table consisted almost entirely of *paisas*, Mexican nationals with no gang affiliation, including my young ex-bunkie, dining together on dorm cuisine.

The next table over were the disciples. They were a handful of unfortunate souls who'd fallen under the sway of another ex-bunkie of mine, Roy. He appeared to be animatedly enlightening them as to the imminent arrival of the aliens to establish peace on earth.

The table beyond that was occupied by a handful of Asians, including my friend Walter.

The table furthest from my Clubhouse, however, is the one, had I not been such a loner, I would have felt truly at home in. This was the eccentrics' table. Holding court there was Pops, whose entire upper body was a massive tattoo. Sitting to his right was Dave, the eternal outsider of the singer-songwriter world, whose courage when performing his music at Camp Taft open mics was legendary, and stood in stark contrast to his mild-mannered demeanor offstage (much like my vulnerable poetry open mic performances during my time before Camp Taft in contrast to my quiet loner-self offstage). And then there was John Michael, who'd written about his experiences with his case in dramatic fashion and shared those writings with me.

I was thrilled to learn in an email from my birthmother, Adele, that my adopted sister Shauna was now president of the Cardiology Technologists Association of British Columbia. I immediately sent Shauna a congratulatory email and told her how I was especially proud of how we both had confounded our mom's expectations for us. But back when I'd been forced to take the plea that would shatter Mom's dreams for me, I hadn't been nearly so proud of myself.

CHAPTER 32

BULLSHIT PLEA

Fall 2012

As time ticked down towards our last drop-dead date, after which we would have to go to trial, my hopes of being able to keep my law license were fading fast. Once Linda's breast cancer had returned, I had been forced to count the cost of what it would mean if we went to trial and lost. And given how much juries hate lawyers, that was a real possibility, as the feds had me on tape telling a client, "Don't let them intimidate you."

"Ladies and gentlemen of the jury," I could imagine the prosecutor saying. "Here we have a textbook case of obstruction of justice. This immigrant client had been lying to federal agents about the work he was allegedly performing to obtain his immigration status. Here his lawyer is encouraging him to continue lying to the federal agents, and not to be intimidated by them."

Her argument would be clear and simple. It would be music to the ears of any juror who'd ever been burned by a lawyer, or who'd had a friend get burned by a lawyer, or who had seen enough crooked lawyers in movies or on TV to believe the story the prosecutor was telling.

Michael A.'s defense would have been far more nuanced and complex.

"Ladies and gentlemen of the jury," I could imagine Michael A. responding. "My client is unlike any other lawyer you've probably ever met. He is very trusting, and was so trusting of Joseph that when Joseph said he'd been falsely accused of immigration fraud, my client, who'd known Joseph for over fifteen years, believed his friend. When he told this immigrant client not to be intimidated, he believed that he was simply protecting his friend Joseph from being falsely accused, by encouraging this client not to be intimidated into lying by the Feds. He had no intention of obstructing justice, as he had no idea this client had been lying to the Feds."

Wow, I thought to myself, *that's an awful lot for a jury to try to wrap their heads around.*

Then one day in the fall of 2012, a few days before my final drop-dead date, I went into Michael A.'s office and sat down so that we could have "the talk."

"What am I looking at if I lose this thing?"

"Five to six years, I'm afraid."

"My God, that would be a death sentence for Linda. And what are the chances I might lose?" I didn't even mention that the prospect of five years in prison would have destroyed whatever fragile psyche I still had left.

"About eighty percent. Remember, they have you on tape, telling a client not to be intimidated by the Feds. The prosecutor's story would be much more believable to most jurors, sadly, than my best defense argument would be."

Now if he'd said sixty percent, or maybe even seventy percent, I might have been willing to roll the dice. But eighty percent was just too great a risk with Linda's life on the line, even for a gambler like me.

"And what am I looking at if I take the plea?"

"Two to three years max."

"I guess you'd better have them make us an offer, then. But remember the three things I will need changed before I can agree to it. First, that I was blind to what Joseph was doing. Second, that I never profited from what Joseph was doing. And third, that when I went to that meeting, I had no idea that the client had been lying to the Feds."

"Okay, Kel, I'll see what I can do."

A few days later, I was over at my immigration lawyer friend Matt's office, helping him out with a case, when Michael A. called.

"She just emailed me her offer. Go check your inbox and get back to me."

I raced over to Matt's assistant's computer, my palms sweating, and checked my inbox.

"Shit, Matt, after three fucking years of stonewalling, she's only agreed to one of my three demands. All she's willing to admit to is that I was blind to what Joseph was doing."

"What else did you want her to change before you'd agree to sign it?"

"That I hadn't profited from what Joseph did, and that I hadn't known the client was lying to the Feds when I met with him and told him not to be intimidated by them."

"Now of those two things, which one can you most easily prove in court?"

"That I didn't profit from what Joseph did. She's saying I made three hundred grand off his eighty-five fraudulent cases. I can prove that I only made three hundred grand total on the fifteen hundred cases we handled during the same five-year period during which those eighty-five cases were filed."

"Then tell your lawyer to tell her you won't agree to the plea until she makes that change. If she knows she'll lose on that one in court, she'll blink."

I then called Michael A. back.

"Okay, tell her this. I can prove that I only made three hundred grand total on the fifteen hundred cases we handled during the same five years Joseph had me file those eighty-five fraudulent cases that he made eight hundred grand on, and his wife made four hundred grand on. So either she admits that I didn't make that three hundred grand on those eighty-five cases, or we go to trial."

"Okay, let's see what she says, " he replied.

Five minutes later, he called me back. "Check your inbox again."

This time her offer had been revised and was accompanied by an Excel spreadsheet. The spreadsheet confirmed what I'd known all along, and what she'd been knowingly lying her ass off about for the past three years. Instead of the three hundred grand she'd claimed I'd made on Joseph's eighty-five fraudulent cases, I'd only made seventeen grand, or two hundred dollars per case. This was the same amount I'd made per case on all fifteen hundred cases I'd handled during that same five-year period.

I called Michael back. "Any chance she'll budge on whether I knew the client was lying when I met with him that day?"

"No chance, Kel. This is the best deal she's going to offer us. Take it or leave it. And her office closes in five minutes, so you'd better decide quick!"

"Trial penalties" are one of the most effective hammers in the prosecutors' tool kit. In my case, that meant go to trial and lose, spend five or six years in prison. Take the plea, spend two to three years max.

It would not be until sometime later that I would finally figure out why the prosecutor had been so willing to admit to my being blind to what Joseph did and to not having profited from it, and yet refuse to admit that I hadn't known the client was lying to the Feds when I met with him. This was because for them to convict me of conspiracy, they didn't need to prove either motive (profiting from Joseph's fraud) or intent (actual knowledge of Joseph's fraud). But for them to convict me of obstruction of justice, they needed to prove intent, that I'd known the client was lying to the Feds when I told him not to be intimidated by them.

After three years of rolling through the seven stages of grief (with most of that time spent in denial) it had all come down to this. I could either roll the dice and take on the Feds with only a twenty percent chance of winning and Linda's life on the line and most likely lose my law license and do double the amount of time if I lost, or I could take this bullshit plea, despite the fact that no one in their right mind would risk a twenty-year career as an immigration lawyer, a career they were passionate about, for a mere seventeen grand. But while taking the plea would mean I would lose my law license and would likely end up going to prison anyways, at least my sentence would be half what it would have been, and so there was a much better chance Linda would still be alive when I got out.

Trying desperately to keep my hands from shaking, I signed the deal that would mean that my old life as an immigration lawyer would soon be over, and scanned and emailed the signed plea deal back to Michael A.

About a week after I'd signed the bullshit plea, and about three weeks before my change of plea hearing where that signed plea deal would be finalized in court, I noticed an email in my inbox from Pepperdine

Law School, my alma mater. I'd stayed in close contact with Pepperdine over the years, volunteering as a moot court judge one year, and volunteering as a mentor to any of their law students who were considering practicing immigration law for the past dozen years or so.

I opened the email and saw that it was invitation to an upcoming talk by another Pepperdine alum, Andre Birotte, who'd graduated from their law school in 1990, the year after me, and who was now the U.S. Attorney for the Central District of California. In other words, this guy was my prosecutor's top boss. I immediately accepted the invitation and thought to myself, *I can't wait to go hear what this guy has to say. If he's as close minded as my prosecutor, it'll probably be a depressing talk. But if not...?*

As I was driving down the Pacific Coast Highway (PCH) out to Pepperdine Law School's magnificent Malibu campus, I left a message for my lawyer friend Tom. I wanted to know what I could, or could not say, to Andre Birotte if I felt courageous enough to try to talk with him after his lecture.

As I was driving past the gorgeous Getty Museum, Tom returned my call.

"You can't discuss any of the details of your case, Kel. You can only ask him hypothetical questions. Be careful, dude. Don't say anything stupid that might blow your plea deal. I know the deal sucks, but if Michael A. says it's the best you can get, you just have to trust that he's right."

"All right. I'll be careful. Thanks!"

I pulled into the law school parking lot a few minutes later and entered the exquisitely familiar law school building. Passing by the library to my left, I descended the stairs to the law school classroom where Andre's talk was about to begin. I was greeted warmly by my old law school Dean, Ron Phillips, who'd written one of my sixty character reference letters, and by the retired immigration and federal judge and current Pepperdine law professor Bruce Einhorn, who'd also written a letter on my behalf, both of which had been ignored by my prosecutor, as had the other fifty eight.

I settled into my seat near the back and watched as a tall, lean Black man strolled up to the podium. I braced myself for what I expected would be another cynical talk, like the one I'd heard at the Marriott hotel a couple of years earlier – where I'd first heard the phrase "sexy headline" – conducted by a prosecutor who assumed that all defendants were guilty and should be taken down by any means necessary.

But I began listening intently when he opened his talk by describing how he'd begun his career by spending five years as a deputy public defender, and that after four years as an Assistant U.S. Attorney, he'd spent another eleven years as a white-collar criminal defense attorney. In other words, he'd spent most of his career defending those accused of crimes, not prosecuting them. As a result, he was surprisingly honest in expressing just how fucked-up our justice system was.

I almost jumped out of my chair, however, when he said, "I'm well aware that confidential informants lie all the time."

Did he just say that? Here was the head of the U.S. Attorney's Office for the Central District of California, the largest such office in the country, with some two hundred and seventy-five prosecutors working for him, publicly acknowledging that one of the key procedures used in a huge number of cases his office handled, including mine, was riddled with fraud.

His underling's case against me, for example, was based on just such a lying confidential informant, the client who'd falsely claimed that I'd known he was lying to the Feds when Joseph and I had met with him at that Barnes & Noble bookstore. The truth was that I hadn't known, and had it not been for that client's false accusation, I would almost certainly have gone to trial and would most likely have won. Without that client's lie, the prosecutor would have been faced with the all-but-impossible task of trying to convince the jury that I had been willing to risk my twenty-year career as an immigration lawyer for a mere seventeen thousand dollars.

Emboldened by Andre's honesty, and truly shocked by his humanity, I strode down to the front after he finished his talk and introduced myself.

"I really enjoyed your talk today. The name's Kelly Giles. I'm a fellow alum. I graduated a year before you, in 1989."

"Very cool, great to meet you. So glad you could make it today."

"Yeah, I just wanted to let you know that there's an abusive prosecution going on in your office."

"Really, which one?"

"Mine. I know I can't discuss any of the details with you, but my prosecutor's name is Elisa F., and my lawyer's name is Michael A. Here's his card."

His eyes never left my face as he took my lawyer's card from me. "Thanks, I'll see what I can do."

I then headed for the exit, my heart racing. At least now I could honestly say I'd tried everything humanly possible to give myself a chance of keeping my law license.

Two days later, I got a call from Michael A.

"What the fuck are you trying to do, blow up the deal? I just got a call from Andre Birotte, the head of the U.S. Attorney's Office here. He said you'd told him the other day that Elisa's prosecution of you was abusive!"

"Yeah, well, sorry about not giving you a heads up. I really hadn't expected I was even going to talk to him when I went to hear him speak at Pepperdine. But I've felt so invisible to Elisa these past three years, and here was somebody who seemed like he might actually care to know the truth about my case."

"Well, Kel, let's get one thing straight here. Elisa's never going to admit that her prosecution of you has been abusive. Unless you're willing to roll the dice with your wife's life by taking this case to trial, I strongly suggest you shut the fuck up and take the deal she's offering you."

CHAPTER 33

FROM MRI AT LAST TO MOVIE THERAPY 101

October 2013

A little more than five months after I injured my Achilles, I finally got my MRI.

"Time to go," called the female guard from the entrance to the TV room. She'd already given me a heads up about an hour earlier, so I was dressed and ready to roll.

She then escorted me down to a barren cell near the entrance to the facility. It was freezing.

"Here, put these on," she said, handing me an orange jumpsuit.

Oh, great, I thought to myself. Any time we were given an orange jumpsuit, it meant we'd be traveling to Bakersfield with at least one inmate from the medium security facility next door. And since they had to be shackled, so did I.

After struggling to squeeze into the way too tight orange jumpsuit (all those rice and beans had been taking a toll), I tossed and turned and shivered in that frozen cell for several hours until jolted to consciousness around 5 am by a male guard yelling, "Let's go, we haven't got all day!"

He shackled my legs together, but at least I got two separate cuffs for my hands, so that I could maneuver my cane.

I shuffled into the rickety old van, nodding at the detainee from the other facility, and off we went in darkness for about forty miles to Bakersfield. These appointments were always for six am so we wouldn't frighten the gentle, law-abiding citizens of the community by our presence. We arrived in pre-dawn darkness and shuffled our way into the doctor's office through a rear entrance.

After about fifteen minutes, I was called in for my appointment, still shackled and cuffed. I felt like a beached whale as I awkwardly attempted to roll over on the examination table.

A female radiology technologist then strolled in and announced, "Congratulations, you've won the Taft MRI lottery," and asked my prison guard escort to unshackle me for the procedure.

Wow, I thought to myself as they MRI'd my right leg, *that officer must be really desperate to have me come work for him, as he knows he can't force me to without these MRI results.*

A half hour later, I was re-shackled and shuffled my way back onto the van. On our way back, the other inmate and I were tossed a couple of brown bags containing slimy mystery meat sandwiches, as we would not be getting back in time for breakfast. The guards, meanwhile, made a pit stop at Carl's Jr., and we watched with envy as they devoured their mouthwatering burgers in front of us.

The MRI results finally came back two and a half weeks later, on November 24th. It turned out I'd only suffered a micro-tear of my right Achilles, though I had also developed plantar fasciitis, bursitis (hence the prolonged swelling), and tendonitis in my right Achilles, and so would need a lot of physical therapy after my release to rehabilitate it.

But I got the last laugh. Because my MRI results didn't come back until a month before my scheduled release to the halfway house on December 23rd, the officer could not force me to come work for him. No one can be forced to work during either the first or last month of their sentence.

It was a Friday evening in early November of 2013. Movie Therapy 101 was now in session.

When I'd arrived at Taft Federal Prison in the spring of 2013, one of the things I knew I was going to have a hard time with was not being able to go see my therapist for ten months. Now as someone who'd spent most of my life trying to avoid therapy, not being able to see my therapist might have sounded like a reward, rather than a punishment.

I naively thought that I might be able to schedule a session with the prison therapist.

Not.

See, I was fooled by the only title that they could fit on his office door, which was Psychologist.

But after submitting request after request to schedule a session with him, and receiving confusing responses asking me what drugs I was currently addicted to, I'd asked my friend Red at lunch one day back in early May what was going on.

"You want a therapy session, dude?" he replied.

"Well, yeah, isn't that why they have a psychologist on staff here?"

"You're shitting me, right?"

"No, I'm serious."

"You actually fell for that job title on his office door?"

"Well, yeah. You mean he's not really a psychologist, then?"

"Oh, he sure is. And a rather well-compensated one, at that."

"Really?"

"Yeah, his job's considered GS-13, so he's gotta be making at least 100k, I'd guess."

"Wow, I really did choose the wrong career. So why does his office keep asking me what drugs I'm addicted to?" I said, pocketing the half dozen sugar packets that had been lying on the chow hall table we were dining at.

"Because his complete job title is Clinical Psychologist Drug Abuse Program Coordinator."

"Ah, then I guess I won't be talking to him any time soon."

"Talk therapy's over-rated anyways, dude. Nature's way better therapy," he said, gazing past me out the window, as if nature's beauty somehow was buried beneath the dust there somewhere.

"Yeah, but ever since I injured my Achilles, they haven't let me go back out to the Native American Garden, which was the only real nature therapy this place seemed to offer."

"True. This desert ain't exactly one of the seven natural wonders of the world. If you can't have nature therapy, the next best thing is art therapy."

"You mean, like all this writing I keep doing?"

"Yeah, but is it helping?"

"Well, yes and no. Yes, as it gives me something to do besides reading. But no, as it keeps reminding me of what a shitty place this is, and that nothing I write can change that reality," I said, sighing heavily.

"Have you ever considered there might be other types of art therapy that might be better able to help you forget where you are?" he said as we walked out of chow hall together and started towards our dorm.

"Like what?" I asked as we started climbing the stairs up to our second floor dorm.

"What day is it today?" he replied.

"Friday. Why?"

"Meet me in the TV room at seven o'clock tonight."

"Ok, see you then."

That Friday night had marked the first time I got to experience the exquisite joys of federal prison movie night. I quickly found that I was far less of a film snob in prison than I'd been on the outside.

On the outside, I went to see mostly foreign and independent films. In prison, sometimes it seemed like the only actors that starred in films any more were Tom Cruise and Denzel Washington.

Then again, context is everything. On the outside, I'd fallen asleep watching *Les Miserables*. In prison, I bawled my eyes out watching *Les Miserables*. In the back row, of course, so none of my fellow inmates could see me crying.

Tonight's film was yet another fine example of the sort of "cinema therapy" that Red had promised, all those months ago, and that the Friday night movie nights had delivered consistently ever since.

Tonight's film was called *Warrior*. Amazingly, neither Tom Cruise nor Denzel Washington appeared in the film. Instead, another actor rather beloved by us inmates, Nick Nolte, played a recovering abusive alcoholic whose two sons, estranged both from him and each other, end up meeting in the finals of an MMA (mixed martial arts) tournament.

The theme in the film that resonated most powerfully for me was that the true warrior spirit can only be found in the power that lies hidden in weakness and vulnerability. While watching the film, I thought about how my adoptive name, Kelly, means "brave warrior".

And how, to try to live up to my name, I'd adopted Bruce Cockburn's "The Strong One" as my theme song: "You help your sisters, you help your old lovers, you help me. But who do you cry to?"

I remembered how a dear friend on the outside had recently helped me own the fact that a wiser, more cautionary theme song for me should have been "Desperado" by The Eagles, as I'd "better let somebody love [me], before it's too late."

Yet I've always been terrified of intimacy. My greatest fear was that I'd end up revealing my weakness and vulnerability, and then would be abandoned by anyone I revealed myself to that completely. Even my wife, if she ever saw just how weak and vulnerable I truly was. One of the weakest, most vulnerable moments of my adult life had been the day I had to go to court to make my bullshit plea official.

CHAPTER 34

WORLD OF SHIT

Winter 2012

Michael A. and I rode up the federal courthouse elevators together in silence. My stomach churned. It was the day I'd been dreading every day for the past three years. I'd fought like hell, hoping this day would never come. But then it had. Without warning. Or with only my worst fears as warning. Linda's breast cancer had returned. Once that happened, the fight went out of me. Why keep fighting, if the risk of losing was five or six years in prison, as opposed to two to three years max if I took the deal?

I'd waved the dirty white flag. Agreed to the bullshit plea. Today I had to seal the deal.

I entered the courtroom and saw two other lawyers already there. Designer Suits. Clearly fat-cats. They introduced themselves to Michael A. One represented Goldman Sachs, the other IBM. Michael A. represented the only live human in court that day.

"We're so sorry to have brought you here today," fawned the government lawyers to their corporate and banker overlords. "What can we do to make this all go away?"

I checked my gag reflex. As soon as I took the stand, the judge asked me, "Were you coerced into taking this plea?"

Hell, yeah! I wanted to scream, but instead I mumbled no.

Sensing my ambivalence, the judge asked a few follow up questions. I mechanically replied. My heart had left the room. I gritted my teeth and lied my ass off.

Once outside the courtroom, I raced to the nearest restroom and threw up.

CHAPTER 35

AUTHENTIC MANHOOD PLAN

November 2013

A year after taking that bullshit plea, and seven months into my sentence, I was still trying to make the best of my time in prison. On this particular night, I did my homework for the "Quest for Authentic Manhood" class I was taking, which was to prepare an Authentic Manhood Plan. The first part of the Manhood Plan was to give voice to what I believed my strengths and assets to be. My greatest strength would have to be the fact that I have been triply blessed, with having had at least three people in my life love me better than I could ever love myself.

The first of these was Pops, my adoptive dad, who simply said "take a deep breath" when I came home with insomnia after having blown my scholarship during my first semester at Pepperdine Law School. I then slept for fourteen hours. Pops had truly loved me back to life.

The second of these was Adele, my birthmother, who searched for me for twenty-six years after having been forced to give me up for adoption when she was an unwed teenager. When she found me, a year after Pops had suffered a traumatic brain injury and after I had fallen into despair that no one could possibly ever love me that way that Pops had, she too truly loved me back to life.

The third of these was Linda, my wife, who had somehow managed to hang in there with me for twenty-one years of marriage, including the past four years in hell since my arrest at LAX and eventual double felony conviction, disbarment, and incarceration, as well as the return of her breast cancer. Without her love and weekly phone calls and monthly visits, I would not have been able to make it through my time here at Taft.

The fact that Pops, Adele, and Linda had managed to love me so much better than I could ever love myself would hopefully give me the courage I was going to need to dive deep into the wounds of my past in my journey to authentic manhood.

The second part of the Manhood Plan was to acknowledge what unfinished business I still had.

This unfinished business began with my having not yet fully acknowledged nor addressed my "silent father" wound from much of the first twenty-five years of my life. Pops, like most fathers of his generation, was away at work for much of my childhood, and left the rearing of my sister and I primarily in the hands of our deeply wounded adoptive mom, who was the only child of an abusive alcoholic father.

It continued with my not having fully acknowledged or addressed my "absent father" wound from the past twenty-five years of my life, ever since Pops' traumatic brain injury half my life ago.

Next came my not having fully acknowledged or addressed my second "absent father" wound. Ever since I was found by my birthmother Adele twenty-four years ago, and she enabled me to reconnect with my birthfather Delwyn, I had been unable to form a true father-son relationship with my deeply wounded birthfather, who was emotionally abused by his tough love father.

Finally came my not having fully acknowledged or addressed my "overly bonded with mother" wound with my deeply wounded adoptive mom.

I was attempting to move through the pain rather than be crippled by it, but it had been, and continued to be, hard as hell, as those wounds cut deep.

I would practically address the wounds affecting me from my past by continuing to watch films and read about the subject, and by continuing to write about all the ways in which I'd come to see my past wounds continuing to affect me in the present.

I would know that I was "finished" with this unfinished business when I could be more fully present and not feel the need to distance and detach myself as a way of trying to bury, deny, or escape my feelings.

I was hanging out in my Clubhouse just now reading Jung's *Meanings, Dreams, Reflections*, when I was struck by something Jung wrote about a manikin and a stone that he'd kept as a sort of secret talisman in his childhood. As I was heading back to my dorm, a stone at my feet suddenly caught my eye. Now Taft is in the middle of the desert, so most of the stones around here are dull and dry and grey. Not this stone, though. It was unlike any of the other stones around. In fact, it appeared to be two stones in one.

At its widest end it was triangular, with the main surface area of the stone slightly wider at the top, tapering down to a slightly narrower base. I should have drawn a picture of it, except that I can't draw for shit. I would have taken a picture of it, except that cell phones tend to be frowned upon in federal prison.

Over eighty percent of its surface was a luminous, milky white, striated with grey parallel lines running horizontally across its jagged surface. At the very bottom edge of the stone was a glittering, rust colored portion that looked like it had been grafted in from a completely different stone.

I felt deeply connected to this rock, flipping it absentmindedly between my fingers as I lay back on my lower bunk bed in my dorm. The striated grey and white bulk of the stone's mass reflected back to me the storm-weary state of my soul, which had spent just over four years now being lacerated. The glittering rust colored base of the stone was for me my battered and bloodied yet unbowed heart, sustained by the flowers grown in GraceLand. My heart had felt especially battered and bloodied during the days leading up to my final merits hearing about a year earlier, and the end of my old life as a lawyer.

CHAPTER 36

FINAL IMMIGRATION COURT MERITS HEARING

December 2012

It was now early December of 2012. I was in the death-throes of my soon-to-be former life as an immigration lawyer, now that I had finally, reluctantly pled guilty to both obstruction of justice and conspiracy to commit immigration fraud.

The California Bar had sent me a knife in the throat letter informing me that, based upon my plea, I would be suspended as of December 7, 2012. This would simply be the first step on the way to my summary disbarment a few months later.

Twenty-three years earlier, in the fall of 1989, I'd received a letter welcoming me to the California Bar. Now, I was to be exiled from the only place I'd felt like I belonged for my entire adult life.

But then, on Tuesday, December 4th, 2012, I got a text message from my immigration lawyer friend Rosana.

"Can you help with a merits hearing with Judge Bank on Thursday at 1?"

My heart leapt to my throat. Could this possibly be happening? My twenty-three-year career would be over this Friday. But before it ends, would I really get to savor one last hurrah in the courtroom?

The day after I received Rosana's text, on Wednesday, December 5, 2012, I had just finished a few morning hearings for her when I saw Immigration Judge Ira Bank, a good friend I had law clerked for when I was just starting out, when he was still a private attorney. He was heading out of the court building on Sixth and Olive right behind me. He waved me over.

"Hey, Ira, how's it going?"

"Never better. What are you up to right now?"

"No plans. I was going to update Rosana on how this morning's cases went, but that can wait. What's up?"

"I'm just heading over to Ralph's to get some food from their deli for lunch. Want to walk over there with me?"

"Sure, I'd be honored to, your Honor. And God knows I could use the exercise."

We proceeded to head south on Olive Street.

"Whatever happened with that bullshit federal court case against you, Kel?"

"I fought it for three years. But when the stress of the case brought Linda's breast cancer back, I quit fighting it and copped a plea."

"I'm so sorry. How's Linda doing?"

"Much better, thanks! She had successful surgery this past spring, and I've been preparing meals and green juices for her."

We turned right and headed west on 9th Street.

"That's great. Yeah, I really wish I could have written a character reference letter for you, but as a sitting judge I wasn't allowed to."

"No worries. Several of my Department of Homeland Security trial attorney friends said they wished they could have, too. But it wouldn't have mattered. I had sixty letters, including one from your recently retired colleague Judge Einhorn, and another from my Pepperdine Law School Dean, but they were all ignored."

"So how soon before the State Bar pulls the plug on you?"

"Two days from now. In fact, I'll be knocking you dead with my brilliant legal analysis for my final merits hearing tomorrow, before I hang up my license for good the next day."

"I'll be sorry to see you go, Kel."

"Yeah, I'm sorry to go. But I'm glad that at least my last hearing will be with you."

By this time we had arrived at Ralph's.

"Yeah, me too. See you in court tomorrow, Kel."

"See you there."

The next day, I won my final case in Judge Bank's court. I congratulated the clients and returned their file to Rosana's office across the street. I then wandered over to Pershing Square and bawled like a baby.

The very next day, my twenty-three-year performance as a U.S. immigration lawyer was officially over. I kept driving and driving up and down Figueroa Street, determined to find free parking, so I would not have to suffer the indignity of both surrendering my law license and having to pay for the privilege of having done so. I should have known better. For despite my having voluntarily accepted my suspension that day, and my disbarment, which would follow some fifteen and a half months later, apparently not even an uncontested suspension and disbarment comes free, it seems. For the California Bar would later find a way to justify sending me a bill for several thousand dollars for the alleged costs of my unchallenged disbarment. Yet just like the unsettled Citibank credit card debt which shall remain forever unpaid so long as I manage to keep all my money in my client trust account, this California Bar debt shall likewise remain forever unpaid so long as I remember to never, ever, get another tax refund again.

After driving up and down Figueroa for the better part of half an hour, a lean brown Lincoln extricated itself from its cozy position next to a parking meter which was glowing with my favorite parking meter color, Irish green. I slid in to see just how much Irish luck I might have on this occasion and was delighted to discover the Lincoln driver has generously offered me an hour of free parking.

I crept down half a block to the dingy State Bar building on the west side of the street and slipped inside. I had no idea which floor the State Bar office itself was on, but the security guard helpfully directed me to the escalator and informed me that the office was on the second floor.

I rode up the elevator, my palms sweating, half hoping that the office might be closed.

No such luck. They were still open. I mumbled my name to the lady at the front desk and sat down on one of the crappy blue plastic chairs in the waiting room. *Wow*, I thought. *With all those State Bar fees we pay every year, you'd think they'd at least get some decent chairs for this place.*

After a few minutes, I heard my name being announced, loud and clear, and took my paperwork up to the clerk's window.

"Tough day, huh?" he said.

"Yeah, that's for sure."

"Well, just remember. Trees that make it through the storm bend but do not break."

"Wow. Thanks, man. That means a lot."

I had no idea who I now was. All I'd ever known were the roles I'd played for others. Now that those masks had all been stripped away, how was I ever going to begin to heal the pain?

CHAPTER 37

FROM SACRIFICIAL LOVE TO DOG HEAVEN TO HEALER OR DESTROYER

December 2013

I had been steadily losing hope of being reinstated into the Christian School of Ministry. Chaplain Colin's refusal to reinstate me had become even more soul-killing of late. In my first round of classes after my suspension and removal, I had been given grades for my papers and had at least been allowed to take the final exam, even if I didn't get a grade for it. In my second round of classes I'd once again been given grades for my papers, but this time had not even been allowed to take the final exam.

Now I was no longer even being given grades for my weekly papers, even though everyone else was. Depression had now descended into despair's lair. No way in hell was I ever gonna be reinstated.

Dave, who'd been a classmate of mine for my first two rounds of classes, came up to me in the Clubhouse and settled in beside me. I'd just finishing mixing up a batch of Kel-Lemonade, with commissary bought lemons and sugar packets I'd stolen from chow hall.

"I asked Chaplain's College to change my religious classification for family reasons a few months back."

"Were they okay with that?"

"No, they weren't. But just like they delayed suspending and removing you for over a month after you'd already quit volunteering in the Native American Garden because of your Achilles' injury, they didn't bother telling me that my requested change of religious classification was grounds for suspension and removal until now, a week before I was supposed to graduate."

"Are they gonna suspend and remove you, too?"

"Hell, no. They said that because I was class valedictorian they would make an exception for me, and would allow me to graduate next week."

"Congratulations! Would you like some of my world-famous Kel-Lemonade?"

"I'd love some, but there's a twist."

"What's the twist?"

"I told them that I could not accept their offer unless they offered you the same deal."

"So then what happened?"

"I suspended and removed myself from the program, and so I will not be graduating next week. I'd rather hang out with you and drink your Kel-Lemonade anyways."

I poured us each a tall glass of my signature drink.

"Principled Rebels of the world unite!" we declared.

"God, I love the smell of desert mud in the evening!" I'd said to my friend Dave later that night on our way to chow hall. After two hundred days of drought since my arrival at Camp Taft, the heavens had finally ripped open, and God had flooded the compound with his pent-up tears of rain.

I hoped that this much needed soaking would be foreshadowing showers of blessing in the dry and weary wasteland of my once productive life. Especially since I'd just found my soul-stone two days before. And especially since Dave had sacrificially offered to give up his School of Ministry graduation in solidarity with my having been suspended and removed.

But hope is a dangerous thing. If the past four years had taught me anything, it was that the only way to never be disappointed is to never have hope.

The desert dogs had returned to Camp Taft today too, after an extended absence. Gruffy and Kilroy, a couple of mutts. Yet way cooler than humans. Growing up, my favorite family members had always been our dogs. They loved no matter what.

I wondered how my two childhood dogs we had the longest, the sable miniature collie Duchess and the blue merle miniature collie

Silver Prince, were doing up in dog heaven. I pictured Duchess rolling around in heaven's massive backyard, while Silver Prince raced madly up and down heaven's seemingly endless sundeck.

The next day, as I gazed down at my right calf, swollen now to twice the size of my left calf, I realized I'd fucked up. I mean, I knew I'd pushed a little too hard trying to run some five-minute laps just now, but I was trying desperately to make up for lost time. Like six months of lost time. It had been six months since I'd injured my Achilles and had not been allowed to work out. Now, though, with less than a month to go until my release to the halfway house in late December, I could finally work out again. Thank God they couldn't make me work during my final month, though.

My balloon-like right leg made me question once again whether I was more a healer or a destroyer. I'd begun my mid-afternoon Achilles rehab workout feeling like I was riding a healing wave of energy. I'd managed to ride this wave through my first couple of five-minute laps.

As the pain persisted and the swelling intensified, my laps slowed. Five and a half minutes. Then six minutes. I realized I was making things worse, not better. I had to quit after just two miles, rather than the four I'd hoped to finish.

Later that night, much later that night, in fact, it was some time around two-thirty in the morning when the guard came and got me and led me down to the barren cell near the entrance to the prison. Nobody in civilized society wants to see us wild inmates roaming around during daylight hours. So, just like with every previous trip to the Bakersfield doctor since I'd injured my Achilles six months earlier, I'd had to huddle in the same barren cell near the front entrance of the prison for three hours, from two-thirty until five-thirty in the morning.

Only now it was early December. This time I'd been left to shiver in the same cell. And, again, just like every previous trip on the Bakersfield Express, I'd had to be orange-jumpsuited and shackled. I was traveling with inmates from the medium security immigrant prison across the way, and the same security measures had to be applied to every inmate that rode in that rickety van.

But boy were those shackles necessary. I was clearly a flight risk as I hobbled and winced, hobbled and winced, as the pain in my severely swollen right calf mocked me for having thought I'd been ready to run four miles the day before, after not having allowed to run at all for the past six months. Once we had made our way through the back entrance of the orthopedic doctor's office in the pre-dawn darkness (fear not, law-abiding citizens of Bakersfield!), I had to repeat the humiliating routine of attempting to maneuver myself onto the examining table like a beached whale while fully shackled.

The orthopedic doctor strode in, and without so much as glancing at my humungous right calf, flipped open my chart, scribbled something on it, and strode back out again.

"I'm in a lot of pain, doc!" I called after his rapidly retreating shadow, as if my words might somehow magically rewrite whatever he'd scrawled on my chart. As I hobbled and winced my way out a few minutes later, the nurse handed me a prescription to take to pill call once I got back to prison.

Motrin. Really? I mean, in the real (non-inmate) world I could have gone down to my local CVS and picked that shit up over the counter. That orthopedic doctor's really earning that hundred and eighty thousand dollar a year salary from the Management and Training Corporation who own and operate Taft Federal Prison.

When I arrived back at Taft and got unshackled by the guard and out of that orange jumpsuit and back into my desert dust colored prison shorts and t-shirt, I barely made it in time for the 7 am count. But by then it was too late. While I'd been shivering in that cell in the holding area from two-thirty until five-thirty in the morning, I'd managed to miss both the three and five am counts back in my cube. Which meant that I, Inmate 57145-112, had apparently escaped. I no longer existed. Since I no longer existed, I could no longer send or receive emails. This must be what the lunatic fringe feels like. Good to know.

Since one of the precious few highlights of my days here at Taft were the half hour each day I could send or receive emails, that meant I would have to spend that half hour trying to replace those lost joys. And so I luxuriated in the shower a little longer than usual. So much longer, in fact, that the hot water ran out and I had to scramble for my towel before I froze.

My worst fear about having re-injured my right calf so fucking painfully was that I might not be sufficiently recovered to be able-bodied enough to get a job at Trader Joe's after my release to the halfway house in South Central. That release date was now just a couple of weeks away. And boy did I need that job at Trader Joe's. While under indictment, I'd heard a former inmate turned author named Charles Shaw (who wrote *Exiled in America* about the parallels between inmates and immigrants) give a talk at the *LA Times* Book Festival about how his first job after doing time had been at Trader Joe's, so I figured they were felon-friendly. I'd already heard from my fellow inmates that the only way to get out of the halfway house early was to work full-time and pay the halfway house a quarter of your salary.

"Dear God, please relieve me from this searing pain," I pleaded. And, miraculously, He did.

Or at least, some combination of God, Motrin, and a dorm which was considerably warmer than the cell I'd been in earlier that day finally brought some measure of relief to my right lower limb.

But as my sentencing hearing had been drawing near, I'd felt there could be no relief from the pain of the end of my old life as a lawyer.

CHAPTER 38

FROM A KIDNAPPING DREAM TO MY SENTENCING HEARING

January -February 2013

On the first Saturday of January, 2013, I went to see my therapist at the Airport Marina Counseling Center, after a two week hiatus for the Christmas holiday. This was the fourth therapist I had been to see in less than a year. The first, my expert witness in what eventually proved to be my unsuccessful battle to keep my law license, had been too mercenary. The second, a graduate psychology student, had been able to mirror my feelings well, but had been unable to be enough of a ladder towards any real growth or healing for me. The third, who had worked with another nonprofit which also offered sliding scale rates for poor folks like me, had been too condescending. Jody, who I was on my way to see that day, was the first therapist I'd been to who I felt could be both a mirror and ladder for me.

About a week and a half before this therapy session, I'd stumbled upon a perfect image for my Christmas e-cards that year. It featured a human peace symbol formed by Palestinian youths in Bethlehem, and the caption indicated that Israeli citizens were planning on forming a human peace symbol in Jerusalem in response at 3 pm that day.

After staying up until 5 am sending the e-card out to everyone on my list, I realized that one person I had not yet sent it to was Joseph. Since Palestinians and Israelis were supposed to be mortal enemies, I felt the message of the e-card compelled me to email it to him, since it was thanks to his betrayal of my trust that I had lost my law license and livelihood and that Linda's breast cancer had returned from the stress of my case after a seven-year absence. I was trying to follow the biblical call to "heap coals of fire on your enemy's heads" – to kill them with kindness, so to speak.

Though his had been the last e-card I had sent, his response was the first I received. Within just a few short hours, he emailed back. "I finally shared with my kids where I will be heading in January. Megan cried a little. Sharon and Justin were okay. Can't wait to see you and Linda again someday. Please forgive what I have done." Where he was heading in just about ten days' time was federal prison, yet he had waited until Christmas morning to share that information with his three kids.

Linda, who was way more in touch with her feelings than I was, went ballistic upon reading his reply, for his having cheapened grace and not repented. I, however, having spent almost my entire life burying my feelings so as not to be overwhelmed by them, had no idea what I felt in response to his reply.

Around a week and a half later, I proceeded to spend the first forty-five minutes of my session with Jody telling him about how I'd reached out to my birthfather Delwyn on Christmas Eve. I'd suffered a leg infection about a year and a half before which, had it gone untreated, could have cost me my leg or even killed me. My birth mom Adele had said that Delwyn suffered from circulation issues in his limbs, which might be hereditary. I had been hoping to enlist Del's help regarding this possibly inherited medical condition which I thought might favorably influence the judge regarding my sentencing. In reality, I was asking him to love me like a father, so I could feel more like I belonged to him. I told Jody how I had been shot down by Delwyn within about five or ten minutes, but that I had then called my foster mom Grace's biological son John, who had talked with me for about forty-five minutes. Not only that, but despite being busy with his own family on Christmas day, John had taken the time to email me nine pictures of myself as Douglas during the first eleven months of my life that I had spent with Grace.

When I'd finally finished my monologue, Jody said, "I feel like there's something you haven't told me about."

And then I told Jody about my email exchange with Joseph.

"He had emailed me back about how he couldn't wait to see Linda and me again someday, and how he hoped I'd please forgive what he had done," I said.

"And how did that make you feel?" he said.

"I honestly don't know."

Having come to understand by then that I rarely knew what I felt until I did some writing, Jody asked me to write out, but not send, what my heartfelt emotional response to Joseph's email would be. I promised him I would try to do just that.

I went home to our condo in Culver City after my therapy session, and, since I could only write outdoors, went out by the pool. Undaunted by the rain pelting down, I crouched in the royal blue and white pool chair, huddled under the royal blue umbrella atop the table which sat three red brick steps above pool level, opened up a vein and poured out my blood-red rage upon the page.

FUCK YOU, FOR FUCKING UP MY LIFE, AND KILLING MY CAREER.

FUCK YOU, FOR FUCKING UP LINDA'S LIFE, AND NEARLY KILLING HER.

FUCK YOU, FOR FUCKING UP YOUR SON JUSTIN'S LIFE, AS HE CAN NEVER BE GOOD ENOUGH FOR YOU.

FUCK YOU, FOR FUCKING UP OUR CLIENT'S LIVES, BY CARING MORE ABOUT YOUR MONEY THAN THEIR FATE.

FUCK YOU, FOR NOT CARING ABOUT ANYONE BUT YOURSELF, MOTHERFUCKER!

All the rage which I had kept so well-contained for over three years came spewing forth onto that page.

My God, how cathartic that exercise proved to be! Our upstairs neighbor David had recommended very early on in this crisis that I start keeping a dream journal. That Saturday night/Sunday morning after I'd completed my rage-filled rant, I dreamt that I had been kidnapped, and that after multiple failed rescue attempts, I had finally been rescued by a soldier.

Now the kidnapping and the multiple failed rescue attempts made perfect sense to me, as that pretty much summed up what the emotional experience of being under indictment for the past three years had been like, especially the countless times I'd seen my hopes that truth and justice might yet prevail end up being dashed once again on the rocks of reality.

But the rescuing soldier was a mystery to me. After all, I was the guy who had accidentally-on-purpose forgotten to register for Selective Service when I had won my green card in the lottery all those years before, and so had had to delay my own application for U.S. Citizenship for a couple of years as a result. And I was also the guy who, while my background investigation to join the U.S. State Department was going on shortly after 9/11, could be found attending every anti-war rally the ANSWER coalition kept sponsoring.

I had also asked one of my neighbors, who works in the entertainment industry, if he happened to know of any filmmakers who might be willing to help me make a micro-budget documentary earlier that same week. My neighbor laughed and said no, but that if I found one, to be sure and let him know. Both questions I'd had about the mystery soldier and about microbudget filmmakers were about to receive a rather surprising answer.

Still pondering my enigmatic dream, I headed off to church at the Vineyard Christian Fellowship Westside that same Sunday morning. While out in the courtyard getting snacks after the service, I overheard a lanky Mexican American Iraq war veteran telling a friend of mine he had post-traumatic stress disorder. I ambled over to join the conversation.

"I overheard you just now saying that you have PTSD. My name's Kelly, and I'm a recently retired lawyer with PTSD," I began.

He said his name was Jason, and he proceeded to tell me how he'd had run-ins with his commanding officers over his refusal to green-light drone strikes which would have killed civilians, which eventually led to his having to get a PTSD-related discharge from the military.

"One of the ways I began to try to heal some of my emotional wounds was by writing poetry. In fact, I'll bring you a copy of my first poetry book, *Swimming in a Thunderstorm*, next Sunday. Hopefully it will help you with your healing journey," I said.

As the conversation continued, Jason began talking about the fact that he was a documentary filmmaker. Just as I had felt compelled to mention my poetry book to him, Jason said, "I've been laying low ever since I got out of the military, just trying to heal. But I feel like God is calling me to help you make a documentary about your story, to help shed more light on your struggles with PTSD."

It suddenly dawned on me that Jason was, in fact, the rescuing soldier in the dream that I had just had. When I ran into that neighbor who worked in Hollywood doing his laundry later that same Sunday, I exclaimed, "Guess what? I found a documentary filmmaker willing to help me make my documentary for free!"

* * * * *

I had previously tried my last immigration court case in the courtroom of my old friend Ira Bank on Thursday, December 6th, 2012, and surrendered my California Bar card to the local state bar office the following day, Friday, December 7, 2012.

Now all that remained was my sentencing hearing. The good news, as my lawyer Michael A. had emphasized as part of his pitch to convince me to accept Elisa the prosecutor's plea, was that the judge could no longer send me to prison for five to six years. The bad news, however, was that he could still send me to prison for two to three years. Given the fragility of my wife Linda's health, as she'd nearly suffered a blood clot when she'd been prescribed tamoxifen after her breast cancer surgery, she and I were determined to do everything we could to try to convince the judge to show mercy.

I called Michael up to see if there might be any creative ways for us to do so.

"Hey, Michael. You remember those spread-sheets Elisa emailed you?"

"Of course. Why?"

"They showed that Joseph made $1.2 million on those eighty-five fraudulent cases, while I made seventeen grand, right?"

"That's right."

"And Joseph was just sentenced to ten months, which is about three hundred days, in prison, right?"

"Right again."

"Since I only made one-eightieth of what Joseph made, then wouldn't a reasonable sentence for me be four days, or one-eightieth of Joseph's sentence? Since I already served eight days in pre-trial detention, shouldn't I be given credit for that, and be sentenced to probation at best, or house arrest at worst?"

"You know how they say that anyone who represents themselves has a fool for a client?"

"Yeah. That's why I'm paying you the big bucks."

"Yeah. A whole three grand more than what you made off this fraud. Maybe we should call ourselves dumb and dumber."

Michael and I had already submitted updated "sentencing consideration" versions of my sixty character reference letters to Judge Wu, who happened to share the same last name as Joseph. Hopefully the judge, unlike the prosecutor, might consider them.

Linda then wrote a powerful, passionate plea to the judge on my behalf. She talked about the recurrence of her breast cancer, as well as about her fibromyalgia and multiple chemical sensitivity. She emphasized the fact that I was green juicing and preparing all her meals for her. She described how lost she would feel if she were left to fend for herself while continuing to work full time. She talked about how her dad had been sent to the Manzanar internment camp during the Second World War, and about how her mom was a Hiroshima atomic bomb survivor. The only edit Michael A. felt he had to make was to remove her additional comment that not only was this the third time that her family had been devastated by the conduct of the federal government, but that I was white.

In addition, another appeal to mercy I'd planned to make was to highlight a near fatal leg infection I'd suffered back in the spring of 2011. When I'd been hospitalized for this, my birthmother Adele had suggested that since my birthfather Delwyn suffered from circulation issues as well, that perhaps it was something genetic. And since American healthcare sucks badly enough outside of prison, and is all but non-existent in prison, I hoped that perhaps a letter from Delwyn might help persuade the judge to grant me probation rather than prison time. But when I called Del on Christmas Eve of 2012, he said he'd only recently developed the circulation issues, that he was sure that my leg infection was unrelated to his circulation issues, and that he'd rather not write a letter on my behalf.

I collapsed onto our living room couch as the line went dead. Here I was, asking my daddy for help in my time of need, and his response was, "You're on your own, kid." Now, with the wisdom of a few more years, I can better appreciate the fact that Del needed to be a full-time dad to his adopted son Derek, which meant that I could not have expected him to be even a part-time dad to me. Derek has suffered far more severely, physically, than I ever have, to the point where complications from his juvenile diabetes had forced him to have quadruple bypass surgery, and he'd had one of his legs amputated below the knee recently from a truly severe leg infection. Given the magnitude of Derek's health issues, Delwyn clearly only had enough emotional energy to be able to care for one truly "beloved son", with that being Derek.

But then I called up my foster mom Grace's biological son, John, once I'd managed to finally pick myself up from our living room couch. My birth mother Adele had helped me to reunite with Grace, and I was looking for a way to reconnect with the little boy named Douglas, which was who I'd been during my first eleven months in Grace's home. After that I'd been adopted and renamed Kelly. I'd always assumed, since my adoptive mom is half Irish, that it was because it was a good Irish name. In fact, my name had been inspired by the fact that the foster home I was adopted from was located on Kelly Street. And John had taken the time to send me several pictures from the first eleven months of my life when I'd been Douglas, being fostered by Grace.

As the sentencing hearing drew near, my lawyer Michael A. and I proceeded to file our pre-sentence brief, along with those sixty updated reference letters. I couldn't wait to see what fresh horrors might be found in Elisa's pre-sentence brief.

Elisa simply could not see me. Despite Michael A. having patiently corrected her misspellings of my first name dozens of times over the course of the three plus years of plea negotiations, Elisa insisted on adding an extra E every time she used my first name in her brief. I was hoping I might later be able to use that as an excuse to invalidate my plea deal, but then I remembered that, unfortunately, the Judge had taken the trouble to spell my name correctly.

But the misspelling of my name was a minor comedic note. Funnier by far was Elisa's repeated references to me as being the sixty-seven-year-old defendant. Apparently my receding hairline, courtesy of my birth father Delwyn, had been enough to convince her that I must be seventeen years older than my actual age.

But then it hit me. Elisa had simply cut and pasted my pre-sentence brief from her most recent successful prosecution of Dan Korenberg for immigration fraud. The only difference between Dan and I was that Dan was guilty. Clearly, however, Elisa simply saw my case as Korenberg, Part Two. The irony of her seeing my case through that frame, however, was magnified by the fact that, some eighteen years earlier, I'd been offered a job by Dan Korenberg, who'd offered to double my salary, but I'd turned him down as I'd heard how unethical he was.

For a moment I regretted not having sold my soul way back then, as at least then my hardcore prosecutor would have had good reason to take me down, and I would have been able to enjoy all that wealth for all those years. But the regret quickly passed and was replaced by a deep sorrow for both Elisa and Dan, who truly seemed made for each other.

Meanwhile, Elisa had saved her greatest Freudian slip until right near the end of her pre-sentence brief. For even though she'd already won her case when she and Michael and the return of my wife Linda's breast cancer combined to convince me to take the plea deal, Elisa wanted more.

Despite having finally conceded that this was a motiveless crime committed by the world's stupidest criminal by admitting that I had been blind to what Joseph had been doing and hadn't profited from it, this victory was clearly unsatisfying for her. So desperate was she to come up with a motive that she managed to create one for me when she wrote (and I quote): "The defendant was motivated to commit these crimes by my greed."

Wow! I remember thinking to myself. *Thank you for making me out to be a far less stupid criminal than I actually was.* For if she had written, as was likely her intent, that 'the defendant was motivated to commit these crimes by his greed', then my having made only seventeen grand on eighty-five fraudulent cases (or two hundred dollars per case), while Joseph made eight hundred grand and his wife May made four hundred grand, would have highlighted how utterly, stupidly small-scale my greed had been after twenty years as an immigration lawyer.

But because she had accidentally told the judge that the defendant had been motivated to commit this crime by her greed, I had now suddenly been elevated to the rank of a criminal mastermind. For in Elisa's alternate universe, despite my having orchestrated the crimes to make it appear as if I were the world's stupidest criminal, my actual motive for committing my crimes was to provoke my prosecutor into accidentally acknowledging her own greed for power.

On the eve of my sentencing hearing, in February of 2013, my foster mom Grace celebrated her 102nd birthday up in Canada. I spent the evening watching the Oscars.

Once the Oscars telecast had ended, I surfed the internet for a while (as what else is one to do on the eve of one's sentencing hearing?) until I stumbled upon the following Oscar Wilde quote from *De Profundis*:

"A man whose desire is to be something separate from himself, to be a member of Parliament, or a successful grocer, or a prominent solicitor, or a judge, or something equally tedious, invariably succeeds in being what he wants to be. That is his punishment. Those who want a mask have to wear it. But with the dynamic forces of life, and those in whom those dynamic forces become incarnate, it is different. People whose desire is solely for self-realisation never know where they are going. They can't know. In one sense of the word it is of course necessary, as the Greek oracle said, to know oneself: that is the first achievement of knowledge. But to recognise that the soul of a man is unknowable, is the ultimate achievement of wisdom."

I fell asleep dreaming of how that quote might somehow sustain me through the events of the following day.

My hope was that the judge would prove himself capable of living a dynamic life by showing mercy and granting my attorney's request that I be sentenced to probation and community service, or to predominantly house arrest. That way, despite the end of my career as an immigration lawyer, I could at least continue being Linda's caregiver as she continued her recovery from her recent breast cancer surgery.

My fear, however, was that he would be content with simply being a judge. As a judge, he would be too afraid of appearing "soft on crime" to allow a lawyer who'd pled guilty to two felonies – conspiracy to commit immigration fraud and obstruction of justice – to walk out of that courtroom with just probation and community service or house arrest. So my solace would have to be that, if he were to sentence me to prison, his punishment would be that he had shown himself to be merely a judge, and in doing so he had lost the ability to aspire to any greater calling than that.

My reward, by contrast, would consist in my no longer being enslaved by my former identity as an immigration lawyer, and to now be free to live a truly artistic life.

My lawyer Michael A. huddled together on one side of the courtroom early the next morning, while my prosecutor Elisa reviewed my file on the other side. In the gallery sat Linda, my mother-in-law Sachiko, my documentary filmmaker friend Jason (who sadly was unable to record the proceedings), and a few other friends.

I stood up next to Michael.

Judge Wu: "Do you, Kelly Giles, accept responsibility for having committed the essential elements of Conspiracy to Commit Immigration Fraud and Obstruction of Justice, as described in your plea agreement?"

"Yes, your Honor. I was negligent in the oversight of my trusted friend and colleague, and deeply regret that fact. I have had to face up to the fact that I acted recklessly and wrongfully and that I broke the law. It has not been simple or easy to accept that I did this. But I now accept the gravity of my conduct and accept that I violated the public's trust."

"Do you accept responsibility for the consequences of your conduct?"

"Yes, your Honor. I have also had to understand the extent to which I let down my clients. I did commit the crimes at hand, but these charges and my illegal conduct comprise a small percentage of the clients I represented. The vast majority of my uninvolved clients have also suffered, having to get new counsel and to readjust their plans. I am heartsick about the difficulties they have faced."

"And do you have anything to say, in addition to your previously submitted pre-sentence brief, with regard to what sentence should be imposed?"

"Yes, your Honor. Accepting responsibility for my conduct has been an evolving process, particularly because part of this recognition has been acknowledging that I have let down my wonderful wife of twenty years. She has felt my pain and suffered greatly. Because she has come to rely on my help with her illnesses, I am disconsolate over the fact that I may not be available to help her at a time when it is so necessary that she be supported. It has not been easy embracing what I have done. I can only hope that those who love me and have relied on me will be able to forgive me, and that I will have an opportunity to again regain their trust. I cast myself upon the mercy of the court."

I then sank down into my seat next to my lawyer. Elisa then rose from her chair one final time.

Judge Wu: "Do you have anything to say regarding what sentence should be imposed on the defendant?

"I do, your Honor. Mr. Giles has been the ringleader of this vast immigration fraud scheme, and, as he himself has acknowledged, has violated the public's trust. He should be sentenced to the maximum sentence available under the sentencing guidelines for the two felony counts he pled guilty to. I therefore would ask the court to sentence him to thirty-three months in federal prison, and that he be fined sixty thousand dollars."

"With all due respect, Ms. Fernandez, you were before me just three months arguing that Mr. Wu had been the ringleader of this immigration fraud scheme, and all the evidence contained in the plea agreement is consistent with that framing. The plea agreement clearly indicates that Mr. Wu and his wife received 1.2 million dollars in proceeds from this scheme, while Mr. Giles received roughly $17,000 in salary from the cases which were part of this scheme. You can only have one ringleader, I'm afraid, and Mr. Wu has already been sentenced to ten months in federal prison as the ringleader of this scheme."

Elisa then slipped down into her seat across from Michael A. and me.

Judge Wu then turned his attention to me. "Mr. Giles, would you please stand while I announce my decision as to your sentence?"

"Yes, your Honor," I replied, trembling as I rose. My stomach churned as I tried desperately to calm my breathing.

"Three months ago, I was very impressed with what a pillar of the community Joseph was, with his strong involvement in his church being especially noteworthy. This then prompted me to make a downward departure in his sentence, from the maximum possible sentence under the guidelines of thirty-three months to just ten months in federal prison, followed by two years of probation, and a seven thousand five hundred dollar fine. I have reviewed your pre-sentence brief and similarly find you to have been a pillar of the community, especially your many years of volunteer work on behalf of Amnesty International. However, I am unable to grant your attorney's request that you be sentenced to house arrest or to probation and community service. Even though you yourself may have been unaware of, and clearly did not profit from, Mr. Wu's fraud, I am sentencing you to ten months in federal prison because you are a lawyer, and so should have been aware of his fraud. This will be followed by two years of probation, and you will also be required to pay a six thousand dollar fine. You will be notified shortly as to which facility you will need to surrender to. Do you accept my decision as to your sentence?"

"Yes, your Honor," I replied shakily.

I then sank slowly down into my chair beside Michael A., fighting back the tears which were welling up behind my eyes.

On the one hand, I was devastated. Ten months of being separated from the love of my life. Ten months of having to trust that our circle of "meal train" friends we had managed to arrange over the past several months would somehow manage to fill the gap while I was away.

On the other hand, I was relieved. Whether it was that the Judge felt empathy for Joseph due to their shared last name, or whether Joseph had conned the Judge just as he had conned me into believing that he was a pillar of the church, the result was that the Judge had shown mercy in sentencing both of us to just ten months rather than the thirty three months the prosecutor had lobbied for. While being given equal treatment with Joseph at my bond hearing almost three and a half years earlier had led to my being sandbagged by a quarter of a million-dollar bond, at least this time around my being given equal treatment with Joseph had worked to my advantage.

As we were leaving the courtroom following the hearing, Linda, unable to contain herself, rushed over to Michael A.

"How could you let this happen?" she pleaded, tears streaming down her face.

"Ask your husband," he gently replied. "He knows what was on the recording of the meeting with the client at the Barnes & Noble Starbucks in Irvine."

And with that Michael A. took his leave.

Our small entourage then ambled across the street to the courtyard located directly between the federal courthouse to the west and the federal building in which I had fought for my immigrant clients for the past twenty-three years to the east. We found a table and pulled up some chairs and let the events of the morning begin to wash over us.

Jason was the first to break the silence.

"When I was a kid growing up in Mexico," he began, "my dad was a missionary. When many of the Mexican farmers my dad preached to became Christians, they decided they could no longer grow crops for the drug cartels. Many were slaughtered for doing so, but I was not traumatized by their deaths, as I knew that they had died for staying true to their God, and that God would reward them for that. Many years later I joined the U.S. Military and was sent over to Afghanistan to help determine whether or not drone strikes should be ordered. When I was ordered by several generals to authorize drone strikes that I knew would kill civilians, I refused, and had to leave the military as a result. Those civilian deaths would have weighed too heavily on my conscience, as they were not "freely chosen" deaths like those of the Christian converts in Mexico. The fact that those drone strikes were ordered despite my refusal to authorize them left me severely traumatized."

As Jason was finishing this story, the judge who had just sentenced me to prison walked by our table and smiled at us. Linda would tell me later she wanted to go punch him. I was so dazed I barely even noticed him.

As Jason told that story, the shock of my prison sentence was still far too raw for me to truly take in its significance. As the shock slowly began to subside, however, I was able to see the parallels between Jason's story and mine. For the generals who had ordered Jason to authorize those drone strikes that would have killed civilians had to blind themselves to the collateral damage of their orders, and their punishment lay in having revealed themselves to be "only generals". Similarly, the judge in my case had to blind himself to the collateral damage to Linda that his sentencing me to ten months in federal prison would create.

For Jason and me, by contrast, our rewards now lay in the freedom we had to live truly dynamic, artistic lives. Jason's documentary story-telling gifts were helping him to break free from the slavery of being "only a soldier." My storytelling abilities would hopefully similarly help me break free from the slavery of being "only an immigration lawyer."

CHAPTER 39

FROM AUTOMATON TO AFFIRMING MY DESTINY

December 2013

I had only twenty-six more days to go in my time at Taft and just wanted to be an automaton for those remaining days. And for the two months after that, when I was gonna be in the halfway house in South Central. All I knew about the halfway house was that at least I'd be back in Los Angeles for the final two months of my sentence. I really, really didn't want to feel the depths of my life's pain right now. I'd had a great gig going as an immigration lawyer and had managed to fuck that up royally. Now I was a disbarred double felon, serving out the final month of my sentence at Taft. And not at all looking forward to the two months in the halfway house that would follow. Life fucking sucked. Being an automaton seemed like the best option for the moment.

But that evening my roommate Six Eight and I were arguing again.

"Why do you always have to break the rules, dude?" Six Eight complained.

"What rules are you talking about?"

"The rule that says we're supposed to keep our bunks neat and tidy or we'll fail the daily inspection," he said, pointing to the pile of books strewn across my lower bunk.

"I'm a writer, man. I need this chaos to create."

"No, you're not, dude. You made any money yet? You a best-selling author just here to do some research?"

I shook my head sadly and began slowly shoving books into one of the boxes beneath my bed. Making a living a writer was but a distant dream, if that. Once I was released to the halfway house in a few weeks' time, I'd need to take whatever minimum wage job I could find, hope-fully at Trader Joe's. I'd then need to pay a quarter of my salary to the halfway house to bribe my way out early. That way the halfway house can get paid for the same bed twice, once for the person who is released to house arrest by paying this bribe, and once for the new inmate who then takes their place in the halfway house.

And then there were those financial commitments I'd had a ten-month reprieve from while I was in prison. Like my car lease payments. Like that six thousand dollar fine I'd been hit with. Joseph had gotten the non-lawyer discount on his fines. I'd gotten the lawyer upgrade.

By the world's standards, now that I'd been stripped of my law license, I was clearly unproductive. But hopefully, as a writer, I'd eventually have something to contribute. I'd learned in one of my Christian School of Ministry classes that voluntary poverty was a spiritual gift of mine. But mostly it felt like a curse. Once I got out I was clearly gonna have to find a way to use my gifts and talents productively enough to pay whatever bills needed to be paid. And hopefully have enough energy left over to pursue my passion as a writer and hopefully contribute that way as well. And then find an agent. And then land a book deal. *Orange is the New Black* meets *Molly's Game.* Coming soon to a bookstore near you.

Then I would finally have an answer for my roommate Six Eight.

Nineteen days later, and a week from getting out of there, on Tuesday, December 17th, we watched Martin Scorsese's *The Aviator,* starring Leonardo DiCaprio as the eccentric billionaire Howard Hughes, for my screenwriting class. When we discussed the film two days later, we rewatched the opening scene where the mother of the young Howard Hughes passes her fears on to him by telling him, "You're not safe." Suddenly I had a vision of my seven-year-old self, although it was a scene that would be replayed throughout my childhood. "Your will must be broken, young man!" my mom screamed at me for having tracked dirt on her living room carpet.

Trouble is, not unlike Howard Hughes, who remained afraid of the world for much of his life, I never really managed to outgrow my seven-year-old self, and spent far too much of my life convinced that my will needed to be broken and molded by those older and wiser than I. Mom seemed to be that older, wiser other in my childhood, while Joseph became that older, wiser other from my mid-thirties through my mid-forties.

Only they weren't wiser. Just older. And just as frightened of the world as I was.

Then later that night in my prayer class, I had another vision. Jesus was on the cross, looking like he'd lost everything. But then, three days later, he transformed that apparent defeat into victory by rising from the dead. Likewise, when I found myself being arrested, and eventually imprisoned, it looked like I'd lost everything. But in reality, I was a "hidden victor", as it took going to prison for me to realize just how dead my soul had become during the decade I'd been working with Joseph.

Finally, with just a few days to go till my release to the Halfway House, I chose to resume reading Jung's *Dreams, Memories, Reflections* rather than the sci-fi novel I was in the middle of. And boy am I glad I did. For as I was doing so, I stumbled upon the part where I identified with what had written about his need to affirm his destiny, and to forge a will that wouldn't break down, but could cope with the world.

From the age of seven through the age of forty-six, I had utterly failed to affirm my destiny, surrendering instead to the destinies of others, like my mom and Joseph. Only once the incomprehensible events of my arrest and imprisonment took place was I forced to affirm my destiny separate from my mom's and Joseph's. I'd been incapable of coping with the world and with fate for four decades. Hopefully through the events of the past four years I was finally beginning to forge an ego of my own, a will of my own, that would enable me to, slowly but surely, transform this apparent defeat into a hidden victory. A little foretaste of that hidden victory had come in the form of a baptismal vision that had been given to the pastor who'd baptized me half my life ago.

CHAPTER 40

FROM BAPTISMAL VISION TO SWEAT LODGE CEREMONY TO LITTLE BOY LEADER

April 2013

Once Judge Wu had finished sentencing me to ten months in federal prison, with my self-surrender date set for two months later, the only remaining question was where I would be spending those ten months. There were only two prisons with minimum security camps in Southern California. The first was in Lompoc, on the coast near Santa Barbara, while the other was in Taft, in the heart of the California desert, just south of Bakersfield.

In addition to breast cancer and multiple chemical sensitivity, my wife Linda also suffers from fibromyalgia. One of the symptoms of fibromyalgia is temperature sensitivity. As a result, I knew just how hard it would be for Linda to come visit me if I ended up at Taft. Yet all the notices I started receiving were indicating that Taft was where they were planning on sending me.

I was lobbying hard to try to be re-assigned to Lompoc instead. Part of those efforts included tracking down and reaching out to a lawyer I'd found in Washington, D.C., who specialized in trying to get prison designations changed. I was considering hiring him for that very purpose when I decided to run the idea by Linda first.

"Hey, hon, all the paperwork I've been getting says I need to surrender myself to Taft at the end of April. I know how hard it would be for you to come see me there, though. I found this lawyer who may be able to help me get transferred to Lompoc instead. Do you think I should hire him?"

"Hell no, Kel. You are meant to go to Taft."

"What are you talking about? Taft's in the desert, Lompoc's on the coast. With your temperature sensitivity, it'll be so much harder for you to come visit me at Taft."

"I know that. But what was that vision the pastor had when he baptized you in the ocean a few months before we met?"

* * * * *

On Easter Sunday, 1990, I was baptized in the ocean down at Venice Beach, California. The pastor who baptized me was brand new to the Vineyard Christian Fellowship Westside, and so had no idea that I was adopted. As he quickly raised my head back up from beneath the surface of the water, the pastor said to me, "God gave me a vision just now of a road going through a desert, with really, really deep foundations. I believe the vision means that you've been wandering through a desert of abandonment your whole life, feeling abandoned by God, and by everyone else, but that the whole time God has been laying down really, really deep foundations of unconditional love for you. I believe that the reason you've been wandering through this desert for so long is to enable you to help others wandering through similar deserts of their own."

That baptismal vision captured powerfully what my life had largely felt like up until that point, and gave me renewed hope that the sufferings I had endured might yet prove to be in service of some higher purpose.

* * * * *

"You mean, the vision of a road, going through a desert, with really, really deep foundations?"

"Yeah, Kel. God was telling you that one day you'd be sent out into a desert of abandonment. That desert is Taft. And by the time God sent you, he would have laid down deep foundations of unconditional love for you."

"But how will you manage?"

"I'm not saying it'll be easy. But we have friends. Your friends from the Vineyard, and mine from the Agape Christian community I once belonged to. They've all signed up on Meal Train to prepare meals for me, and several have offered me rides to come see you. Since God has called you to Taft, God will simply have to give me the strength to come visit you there."

A couple of weeks before I was scheduled to surrender myself to Taft Federal Prison, my neighbor Brian offered to take me along with him to an invitation-only sweat lodge up in the hills near Malibu. Pops was part First Nations, with some Metis blood, and I had been fascinated by Native American spirituality ever since Pops had told me about that part of his heritage when I was a child. We picked up some tobacco as our gift to the ceremony's host and headed off down Pacific Coast Highway in Brian's car. I watched as the slowly setting sun played hide and seek with the late afternoon fog. We arrived around 6 pm and were surprised to find that they had barely begun building the sweat lodge, and disappointed to learn that they had decided to cancel the ceremony as a result. Just as we got there, however, a Lakota elder arrived from New Mexico, and insisted that the ceremony take place.

Even though over half of us had never participated in a sweat lodge before, let alone built one, we followed the lead of the veterans and set to work. We stripped the willow saplings and bent them together to begin slowly constructing the frame, and after several hours of strenuous labor, we finally managed to complete the task. As we began preparing ourselves for the ceremony, the Colombian host of the ceremony told us, "We spent several hours searching for these willows earlier today. Just as we had begun to despair of ever finding them, we prayed one last prayer, and just around the next bend managed to locate the grove of saplings which enabled us to be able to build today's sweat lodge after all."

As the ceremony began, the intense heat from the blazing coals in the center of the lodge was so overwhelming that I had to fight back my burning desire to flee. Just then, we began to sing a series of sacred songs, and my mind somehow floated from its fear of being overpowered by the heat to the bliss of being a part of this sacred ceremony.

Midway through the ceremony, we were encouraged to share whatever prayer requests were on our heart. I shared my fears about having to head off to federal prison in a couple of weeks' time. Our Colombian host replied by singing a heartbreakingly beautiful sacred song which means "Morning Star". The lean Lakota elder, sitting to my immediate right, had earlier told me that he had "never met as many beautiful Indians as he had in federal prison." He too began to sing an achingly gorgeous sacred song. Halfway through he broke down weeping. I wept too. I felt so deeply loved and cared for by someone I'd only just met.

About a week after my first sweat lodge ceremony, and just over a week before I had to surrender myself to Taft Federal Prison, my home church friends managed to convince our church's pastoral staff to grant me a "street kid scholarship" to attend our church's men's retreat. I call it the "street kid scholarship" because back when I was a kid growing up in Victoria, Phil Troop, who ran the Mustard Seed Mission, used to sponsor a homeless street kid from the Mission to go to the summer camp I went to each summer up at Half Moon Bay, near Nanaimo, on Vancouver Island, British Columbia.

I always befriended those street kids, as I just found them to be way cooler and more real than the other kids up there. One of my favorite street kid friends was a wiry kid named Sammy. Sammy used to love to get in the face of the "party six nights and go to church on Sunday" kids at camp and say, "Are you a Christian?" When they would sheepishly reply, "Well, yeah," he would fire back with, "Well then, act like it!" I loved that authenticity, as it forced me to begin asking myself those kinds of questions, too.

* * * * *

I pulled my dusty black Acura TSX into the parking lot of the In-N-Out Burger near Valencia to meet up with a few of my friends on our way up to the Westside Vineyard Men's Retreat at The Oaks, which was located up near Lake Hughes, California. I had already Google mapped the directions to Taft Federal Prison, where I would be surrendering myself in just over a week's time. I knew that I would be taking this same route that day, but then continuing north on the I-5 for another eighty miles. Ironically, I would end up celebrating my "last meal of freedom" at this very same In-N-Out Burger on my way to Taft. On this fabulous Friday, however, ten days prior to that morbid Monday, I was about to surrender myself to a weekend long spiritual retreat. This would be far shorter than the ten-month spiritual retreat I had told the *Los Angeles Times* was my reason for cancelling my subscription, shortly before making my way up to Taft.

Shortly after our In-N-Out feast, we made our way the final few miles to our rustic retreat at The Oaks, nestled in the forest near Lake Hughes. I've always loved forests, from the one behind our childhood home in Victoria where I'd built my first treehouse to the ones surrounding Beaver Lake where I'd spent so many summers with my best friend Alan, to the ones I'd hiked through and camped in throughout my growing up years.

Hiking in the forest helped remind me that nature's rhythms were so much slower and more peaceful than the frantic, chaotic pace I'd been living in the city. As I hiked along the lush green hills throughout the weekend of the retreat, I managed to forget for a moment the baked brown and grey desert prison I'd be lumbering through in the very near future.

After my hike, I sprawled out on the grass and did a little writing. As I scribbled away, I soon found myself writing about four major "head traumas" I'd been through in my life: my "near nervous breakdown" during my first semester at Pepperdine Law School in 1984, my arrest at the Los Angeles Federal Building shortly after the Oklahoma City bombing in 1995 when I was emotionally abused by a cop, my arrest at LAX in the fall of 2009, and my change of plea hearing in the fall of 2012, when I'd finally been forced to accept the end of my former life as an immigration lawyer.

That same Saturday evening, a guest speaker gave a talk in the auditorium, after which we were asked if any of us wanted to come up for prayer. Given that I'd been going up every Sunday for the past three and a half years for after-service prayer (as there are no atheists under federal indictment), I went up not once, but twice, for prayer on this night.

The guest speaker, as he was praying over me, said that God had given him a vision of a little boy longing for his daddy's love. Given that I had felt fatherless ever since my adoptive dad's traumatic brain injury from a near-fatal car crash during the first semester of my last year of law school in the fall of 1988, that vision sounded about right.

The second guy who prayed over me, however – one of the members of our church's regular prayer team – said that God had given him a vision of a leader. That vision made no sense. I had never, ever thought of myself as a leader. In fact, that was a big part of Joseph's power over me. Joseph had always seen himself as a leader. Joseph had also made clear to me what my role was, which was to be his loyal "fireman", someone who remained cool in a crisis, and who was able to solve any issues our immigrant clients might have. This was a role I was quite content to play, as it meant never having to worry about being a leader myself.

That night I had a dream. In that dream, it became clear to me that in addition to the four "head traumas" I'd written about earlier that day, I'd also suffered at least three major "heart traumas" over the course of my life. Those included being torn away from my birthmother Adele and cast out into the cold of the Burnaby General Hospital nursery when I was born, being ripped away from my foster mom Grace eleven months later and taken to the strange new world of my adoptive home, and losing Pops to that TBI when I was twenty-five and searching for a father ever since. I awoke the next morning feeling raw, with all those painful memories rippling through my storm-tossed mind.

During that final Sunday morning service, we were all asked whether there was anything we felt God had put on our hearts to share with the group. This young red-headed guy I'd never seen before, on the far side of the auditorium, raised his hand and said that God had given him the verse Proverbs 24:16, which said, "The righteous man shall fall seven times, and rise again. The wicked shall fall once, and be destroyed."

As soon as he shared that verse, I knew that it was meant for me. The "seven fallings" in the verse were the seven "head and heart traumas"

I'd either written or dreamt about. And the "rising again" was a promise that I, too, would eventually somehow manage to "rise again" from my most recent falling.

I raised my hand. I went up to the front. I babbled incoherently. I bawled like a baby. As soon as I got done with my sob-fest, I couldn't wait to get the hell out of that room. I made a beeline for the exit.

I had never been that emotionally naked in front of a bunch of guys before. I had rarely been that emotionally naked ever. The last thing I wanted was to be around anyone else right then.

I filled my lunch tray in the cafeteria, and then made my way out on the sundeck to an empty table and began eating. My friends from my home church, who had lobbied the pastoral staff for my "street kid school scholarship" so I could come up to this retreat, gave me my space. As I was finishing off my dessert, though, they gathered around in a gesture of solidarity. One of my closest friends in the group, a guy named Larry, who'd done time in both prison and rehab, broke the ice.

"Thanks for what you shared just now, Kel."

"Are you kidding? I was just babbling."

"No, dude. When I was in AA, I used to love it when guys would be vulnerable like you were a few minutes ago. It gave the rest of us permission to do the same."

"Thanks, man. That really means a lot to me."

Maybe, just maybe, I thought to myself, this was one small example of how I might yet find a way to be the "little boy leader" God seemed to be calling me to be.

CHAPTER 41

FROM BOLDLY CHALLENGING AUTHORITY TO A LITTLE MORE HUMAN

December 22, 2013

It was December 22nd, 2013. My adventures in Taftghanistan were finally ending. For the longest time now, it had felt like this sad little routine would never end. Yet now it was about to. Tomorrow I would be heading off to my new adventures in the halfway house in South Central Los Angeles.

I had given my friend Zachary my first poetry book, *Swimming in a Thunderstorm*, as so many of the poems in there had resonated for him. I had donated my other two poetry books, *Surfing the Tsunami* and *Surrendering to Transcendence* to the prison library, in exchange for an out-of-print book I'd been unable to find on the outside, *The Last Western*. Even though the prison librarian had verbally authorized the exchange of books, I was terrified as I huddled in the cell awaiting my release that they would search my belongings, accuse me of trying to steal the book, and deny my halfway house request.

Thank God they didn't. Instead, a couple of the guards drove me out to the Taft bus stop with my boxes of belongings and left me there. As I waited for the bus, I remembered fondly the handful of people who'd helped humanize my stay. Like Nurse Janine, the only prison staff member to treat me as fully human. Like Severin, my spiritual mentor, who'd affirmed my heart for the lost and my willingness to boldly challenge authority when he prayed me out during the last chapel session before my departure. Like Red, who helped me learn to stand up for myself. Like eBay, who'd sung "Happy Birthday" to me and helped me feel less alone.

I took the bus from Taft to Bakersfield, where Craig O'Connor, my friend from our Westside Vineyard Church, was waiting for me, along with Linda. Linda and I embraced, we loaded my boxes of belongings into Craig's car, and headed south. Once we reached Valencia, we stopped at the same In-N-Out Burger I'd enjoyed my last pre-prison meal at. That "3 x 3 animal style" with the pickles on the side for Linda and fries and a strawberry shake tasted like heaven.

We then drove the rest of the way down to South Central Los Angeles, and I unloaded my boxes of belongings at the entrance to the halfway house. Linda and I embraced once more, and I got ready for my next adventure. I hoped to start feeling a little more human again, after being treated like an infant for most of the past eight months.

CHAPTER 42

COEXISTING WITH CHAOS/LIFE AFTER PRISON

There was only one way to shorten your federal prison sentence, which was to agree to go to a halfway house. I had immediately offered to do so upon my arrival at Taft, and now my wish had been granted. I would be spending the final two months of my sentence at a halfway house in South Central.

I didn't get the reality of the "scarlet F" until I tried to get a job at Trader Joe's, and, after being told they would get back to me in thirty days, was turned down just three days later.

After eight months of experiencing a thousand and one ways to consume rice and beans, I was convinced that prison food must be the worst food imaginable. I could not have been more wrong. The foul-smelling, slimy mystery meat inserted between two slices of moldy white bread which was the height of halfway house cuisine took me to whole new levels of food horror.

Not only was the food even worse than in prison, but the accommodations were much, much worse. Instead of a three- or four-man cube, there were around twenty of us crammed into bunkbeds in a single bedroom. One person would start coughing, and we'd all get sick. One person would insist on keeping the fan on all night, and we'd all freeze.

I had to find a way to escape. And there was only one way out. Work full-time and pay the halfway house one quarter of your total earnings for the entire length of your sentence. Only then could I be eligible for release a few weeks early.

So that's what I did. I called up three of my immigration lawyer friends. I begged them to let me come work for them. None were able to employ me full-time, so I worked for all three to work the equivalent of one full-time gig. I insisted that they pay me minimum wage. There was no way in hell I was gonna give those halfway house fuckers any more than the minimum necessary to bribe my way out of there. Ok, they wouldn't call it a bribe. They'd call it the "rules" for halfway house eligibility. Corporations are so much better at covering up their criminality with a veneer of legality than us mere mortals.

At this point, I didn't want any visitors, even if visits were allowed. I was rarely there, anyways, spending up to fourteen hours a day commuting and working my three jobs.

I was also smart enough not to have my car there. Nobody parked their car in South Central. The one person at the halfway house who did awoke the next day to find their battery had been stolen. Commuting to all three jobs required public transit. For the downtown and Culver City jobs, no big deal.

For the Orange County job, much bigger deal. Six or seven transfers between Metro lines and buses. Missing one transfer would mean adding an hour to my commute. The days I worked the Orange County job, I would commute six to eight hours to work my six hour shifts.

Once I'd been exposed to the fine dining of the halfway house in South Central, I was thrilled to spend twelve to fourteen hours a day commuting and working to escape its cuisine a few weeks early.

There were, however, two positives to my halfway house stay. The first was that I'd always wanted to go to a Black church. Since the weekend passes were too short for me to commute all the way to my home church in West Los Angeles, the only church within walking distance was a wonderful Black church. I felt right at home there, from the moment I walked in, and when not just the congregation, but the pastor too, were all singing and dancing throughout the service, I thought, *This must be what heaven feels like.*

The second positive was that while I'd heard conscious hip-hop before my time in South Central, I now understood it in a way I never had before. Unlike most commercial hip-hop, much of which is produced by the same corporations that own the private prisons and halfway houses (once again, a brilliant business model, to push music on the front end which romanticizes the very lifestyles that will help fill your prisons and halfway houses on the back end), conscious hip-hop was expressing a lived experience that I had only now found myself being briefly exposed to.

One thing that didn't change between the halfway house and house arrest was the 10 pm curfew. One night after I'd gone out after working my job in Culver City, I'd managed to miss my 9 pm bus, and, realizing that if I waited for the next bus I'd be late for curfew, I called my friend Mark and he drove me to the nearest Metro Station, enabling me to make it back to the halfway house by 9:59.

Finally, in the first week of February of 2014, Linda came and picked me up, along with my boxes of belongings, and I graduated from the halfway house to house arrest. My workdays in Garden Grove improved the most, as I went from a six to eight-hour daily transit commute to about an hour and a half round trip by car.

I got used to having my sleep interrupted by all the late night and early morning calls to confirm I hadn't violated my curfew, as that was a small price to pay for finally being able to enjoy the comforts of home once again. The 10 pm curfews remained entertaining, as one night I had a chance to go to a free screening of *Before Midnight* which started at 8:30 pm, and found myself having to leave midway through to make it home before curfew.

From the three jobs I'd needed to qualify for early release, once the final three weeks of my halfway house sentence I'd spent under house arrest were completed, I was now working just two. The lawyer whose office was downtown wanted me to stay on full-time, but to do so for minimum wage. Old me would probably have done just that. New me said *hell, no*.

Matt, my friend in Culver City, offered me work three days a week for twenty dollars an hour, which was great because his office was just a few minutes from our home. Mina, my friend in Garden Grove, offered me work two days a week for twenty-five dollars an hour, as her office was a much longer commute.

I was working on mostly religious worker cases at Matt's office, which I really enjoyed, as I had always felt like being a lawyer had been my ministry. To help others fulfill their spiritual callings in ministries that may not have been traditionally considered ministries (Youth With A Mission, for example, even has a surfing ministry), was truly gratifying.

Mina's job offer was especially compassionate as she really didn't have all that much work for me but felt so bad about what I'd been through she did all she could to keep me employed.

Unlike Germany, where I would still be a lawyer because I didn't know what Joseph was doing and did not profit from it (no motive nor intent), our legal system is very Old Testament, as it is "retributive", rather than what Jesus calls us to in the New Testament, which is "restorative" justice.

Right before I gave a talk in the September of 2014 to a USC law school class (a sneak preview of my upcoming memoir) called "Heart Surgery for the Legal Profession", I happened to see, on a screensaver at Matt's law office where I was working, a definition of "retributive justice" which shocked the hell out of me: "punishment that is morally right and legally justified". Now while losing my law license, livelihood, and liberty may have been "legally justified" under our retributive legal system's definition of "conspiracy" (no motive or intent, but rather "strict liability for lawyers"), it was NOT morally right, as evidenced by the fact that I would still be a lawyer in Germany. The absurdity of what happened to me was captured beautifully by a law student/stand-up comic (a perfect side gig for any aspiring lawyers, by the way) who said, at the end of my talk, that the fact that I was white and a lawyer and yet even I was afraid of the law was pretty fucked up.

And that was my twenty-minute talk, my 250-page memoir, in a single one-liner.

Jesus was NEVER willing to settle for retributive justice, hence his handling of the woman caught in adultery incident, when he challenged her accusers by saying, "Let he who is without sin cast the first stone."

Jesus calls us to seek to change our fallen, very Old Testament retributive justice system with a truly restorative justice system. And one shining example of restorative justice would soon be demonstrated to me by my probation officer, just a month after I gave that talk to those law students.

I didn't get how potentially soul-destroying probation could be until Pops was nearly killed in yet another car crash in Canada in October of 2014, and I found myself facing the possibility of not being able to go see him, as I couldn't leave the Central District of California and had been forced to surrender my Canadian and U.S. passports until the end of my probation. Thank God I was blessed with a probation officer with enough of a heart to convince the judge to let me go to Canada, and to convince the State Department to issue me a new passport, so I could go see Pops after his second near fatal car crash.

I couldn't sleep. Just like I couldn't sleep my entire first semester at Pepperdine Law School after realizing I'd blown any chance of renewing my scholarship. That insomnia had marked the beginning of the end of my Smart Kel facade.

Just like I couldn't sleep the night after my arrest at LAX. That sleeplessness had marked the beginning of the end of my Lawyer Kel facade.

But this sleepless night felt strangely different. It felt like both the beginning of the end of something, but also like the beginning of the beginning of something completely different.

Linda and I had flown up to Abbotsford, British Columbia, Canada, a few days earlier to spend time with Mom and Pops, both of whom had been nearly killed in a car crash when Mom's blood sugar crashed while she was driving. We were gonna be flying back to LA the next day.

Unable to sleep, I searched for something to occupy my racing mind, and my eyes locked on an overdue library book I'd brought up to Canada with me, John Gardner's *On Becoming a Novelist*. On pages 50-51, I was struck by how he talks about writers as being childish, and of being unconcerned with the things most grownups care about – like money, power, the flag – but instead just wanting to make art.

Suddenly it hit me. I'd been called to be a writer. That still, small voice in the back of my head, which had been there since I wrote that first letter to the editor of the *Victoria Times-Colonist* at the age of seven, about integration being a wonderful thing as we could learn so much from other cultures, had never, ever gone away, no matter how much I'd tried to silence, or ignore, or run away from it. In fact, I'd run away from it so persistently that, much like the biblical character Jonah, instead of being swallowed by a whale, I'd had to be swallowed up in the belly of the federal prison system before I could finally come to my senses. That still, small voice was now ringing out loud and clear. I'd seen how writing had saved my life countless times, but only now was I finally beginning to see that it had been my true calling all along.

After checking in with Pops, who had miraculously survived an aortic tear to his heart, I had a few minutes alone with my mom as she lay in her hospital bed the next morning. I leaned over to her and said, with all the courage I could muster, "You know what, Mom? I was called to be a writer, and I kind of got lost there for a while as a lawyer."

And there it was. Thirty-five years earlier, Mom had dismissed my expressed desire to be a hotel manager after I'd learned in my Careers class that I'd make a great one, with the words, "You don't have to go to college to be a hotel manager." I had shut down my dreams from that moment on and deferred to hers.

Now, at long last, I'd finally found a dream of my own.

And yet another fine example of restorative justice had been my Vietnamese immigration lawyer friend Mina, who was so sacrificially restorative in her employment of me that she kept me working a couple of days a week for over a year and a half after my release from prison, with my primary job title being simply "resident artist" without any clearly defined job duties.

I'd always sensed a deep gentleness about Francesca, a new young Filipino lawyer who had recently started working at Mina's office, too. Then came the Friday when Mina had emailed me to say she could no longer afford to keep me on. I'd been too distraught to respond that afternoon, but Francesca, who'd noticed my silence, in sharp contrast to my usual more talkative self when I would be there, came up to me near the end of the day.

"How are you doing?" she asked.

"Devastated. Mina emailed me today to say she can't afford to keep me."

"I bet it's just a misunderstanding," she said. Her words gave me hope that weekend. So instead of just curling up in a ball, I reached out and offered my services to a number of my other immigration lawyer friends and ended up landing another job as a result. Not only that, but Francesca's words proved prophetic, as it turned out Mina did have work for me after all, but mistakenly thought I was no longer interested in being a law clerk.

So instead of losing my part-time gig there, I ended up becoming both a law clerk and a mentor to Francesca for the next several months. The best thing about doing so was that, unlike my other two law clerk jobs, which are much more of a "partnership of equals" with my other two immigration lawyer friends, with Francesca I got to be a mentor again and share some of my hard-earned wisdom with someone just getting started in the field. Prior to my arrest, I'd been mentoring Pepperdine law students for several years, but once I caught my case, they were no longer interested in having me be part of their mentorship program.

From the pain of losing that long-time Pepperdine mentorship gig had come the joy of getting to be a mentor to Francesca. I especially loved how appreciative she always was of whatever help or wisdom I was able to offer her, and of just how deeply compassionate and empathetic she's always been.

Then one day Francesca told me she was leaving. She'd accepted an offer from the Immigration Service to begin working as an asylum officer at month's end. I was heartsick. I missed her dearly when she left the following week, as while great lawyers may be readily replaceable, great humans like Francesca are priceless.

So instead of being down to just one part-time law clerk job, I was back to having three. The most challenging, and therefore the one that made me made me feel most like a lawyer again, was my newest job in Glendale working with Donna. In that job I was back to doing what I'd loved the most during my first decade as a lawyer, writing legal briefs for immigration court and even federal court that could potentially save the lives of our immigrant clients. In the case that I'm proudest of, in fact, I did just that. I prepared a humanitarian parole case for a female women's rights activist in Afghanistan and obtained an expert opinion letter from Amnesty International's Afghanistan country specialist, which I was able to get because of the relationships I'd cultivated in over a decade of volunteering with Amnesty at concerts. When we won that case, she was able to find safe haven in the United States, and no longer have to live in constant fear of the Taliban's death threats.

My second most challenging job was the one with Mina, where she now also had me back to doing what I'd loved the most during my first decade as a lawyer, writing mostly political asylum legal briefs for immigration court that could potentially save the lives of our immigrant clients. Her asylum clients were mostly Middle Eastern, where there were many ways one's life could be in danger from the government, including being gay, having the wrong religious beliefs, or making art that's critical of the government.

The least challenging, but equally fulfilling, job was the one with Matt. It was less challenging because preparing mostly religious worker cases involved mostly clerical work, but it was equally fulfilling to be able to help our clients fulfill their spiritual callings, just as I'd always felt that helping immigrants was my spiritual calling.

I was startled from sleep one morning by my cellphone vibrating from a text message from Donna, the immigration lawyer in Glendale I was clerking for.

I then called her right back.

"Why didn't you work on Andy's brief?" she demanded. "It's due this Monday. Instead you worked on a simple case and another one that is not even urgent. Do you expect me to work on Andy's brief all weekend?"

"Andy's case was dismissed," I replied, as calmly as I could. "The one case I worked on was due today, and I had no idea the other case was no longer urgent."

"Andy's 2017 case was dismissed. Not his 2016 case."

"His 2016 case was already dismissed last year. All we have left is his 2017 case."

"You should have called."

"I'm sorry. I should have called. If you want me to work on the brief tomorrow, so you have something to show the client, I'll be happy to do so."

"I don't care about the client. I care about the deadline."

"There is no deadline. The case was dismissed. If you think I'm wrong, I can come in today and work on the brief. I'll just have to let Matt know."

Silence.

"I have to let Matt know. Do you want me to come in today, or tomorrow?"

"I have no idea as I am at a hearing. I have not had a chance to look. I don't know what brief is due July 10th. I know nothing. I was relying on you."

"Ok, I believe Andy's brief is no longer due July 10th, as both his petitions for review have now been dismissed. I will go to Matt's today. If you still want me to prep Andy's brief, I will prep it Friday."

Remembering the words of Ira Bank, the first immigration lawyer I'd ever clerked for, some twenty-eight years earlier, to "bring me solutions, not problems", I then sent Donna one final text message.

"Rather than a now unnecessary brief, I believe I should prepare a Motion for a Stay of Removal tomorrow. And you may want to ask the client if he wants to go to the press."

Wow, I thought to myself almost twelve hours later when I wrote these words. *I'm finally starting to get a little better at not being sucked back into the chaos of other people's prisons of fear. The old me would not have had the strength to stand up to Donna, just as the old me had never had the strength to stand up to either my adoptive mom Pat, or to Joseph. The new me not only stood up to Donna, but made it clear to her that I was standing up to her for all the right reasons, which was to not do any unnecessary work, but rather to focus my energies only on doing work that would actually serve the client's best interests.*

Then the very next day, Donna texted me again. "Don't bother coming in today. I'm working on an emergency motion on another case, and haven't had a chance to call Andy yet."

At first, I was disappointed that I wouldn't get paid sixty dollars for the afternoon's work, but then I recalled that stressful series of texts from a day earlier and reminded myself that at least I wouldn't have to drive an hour through Friday afternoon traffic to work three hours to then drive another hour through Friday evening traffic, all for just sixty dollars.

And just then God decided to have a little fun with me. I called back a couple of prospective Canadian immigration clients who had left messages for me earlier that day. When it turned out that one of them was a dual Canadian and American citizen, and that because he was a Canadian citizen he need not worry about any minor criminal charges he might have had in the States causing him any problems returning to Canada, he was so relieved and appreciative that he insisted on paying me for my consultation. It had been less than five minutes, I said, and so I felt I really couldn't charge him more than fifty dollars. *No*, he insisted, *I want to pay you a hundred dollars.* And so God had the last laugh that day. For while I had missed an opportunity to make only sixty dollars for five hours of my time, God found a way to reward me with a hundred dollars for just five minutes. The contrast being merely needed and used on the one hand, as opposed to being loved and appreciated on the other, could not have been any clearer.

At the time all of this happened, I'd never heard of the concept of "trauma bonding," which is when the intermittent reinforcement of reward and punishment (like my being rewarded by Joseph with a feeling of belonging for being a good fireman, and punished by him with shame and guilt whenever I would consider leaving either him or his clients behind for my own good) create powerful emotional bonds that are resistant to change. Without my realizing it, these bonds had made me physiologically addicted to Joseph's abuse. Most victims will return to their abuser about eight times before they are able to leave. In my case, I was similarly blind to countless red flags, and so kept returning to Joseph and/or his clients time and time again.

The whole time I was working, I was also taking Memoir classes at UCLA Extension and the Writing Pad, just as I'd taken writing classes throughout my twenty-three years as an immigration lawyer. I was also driving up to Santa Barbara every month to workshop my memoir in progress with a writer's group of mostly sci-fi novelists I'd met at the first Santa Barbara Writers Conference I'd gone to in June of 2014, just four months after the end of my halfway house/house arrest sentence. I'd picked Santa Barbara over San Diego or San Francisco by default, as it was the only one of the three big California Writers Conferences where you could meet with agents that was within the Central District of California, which is the only place I was allowed to be during the two years I was on probation after the end of my halfway house/house arrest sentence. Thank God I did, though, as that writer's group helped me finally begin to feel like I belonged as a writer.

CHAPTER 43

DR. KEL-DAR 666: OR HOW I LEARNED TO STOP WORRYING AND LOVE THE BEAST

One day after my probation had ended and I was free to travel up to Canada, Linda and I had flown up for a visit with my families and I was talking with my adoptive mom Pat about God.

"You know," I began, "remember when I told you about our childhood next door neighbor Ozzie telling me that Pops had often told him that his God was too big for any church to contain?"

"Yeah…"

"Well, you also know how Jesus said that when you help the least of these, you're helping Jesus, right, and that those who helped the least of these would also be welcomed into heaven?"

"Okay…"

"Well, I feel like my Buddhist friend Mina keeping me on her payroll even before she had work for me was helping the least of these, and therefore helping Jesus, and therefore she'll be welcomed into heaven."

"Sure, she may have been helping Jesus, but you know that only those who accept Jesus as their Savior are going to heaven, right?"

"I don't know that. I believe I will see my Buddhist friend Mina in heaven. Joseph, on the other hand, claims to have accepted Jesus as his Savior, but the way he betrayed me for money showed that his true god is money. I'd say Mina's much more likely to be in heaven than Joseph is."

"Wow, son. You'd better be careful saying things like that. You're sounding an awful lot like the Antichrist."

"Really? Well, look at the time. I think Adele's expecting Linda and me for a visit right about now."

CHAPTER 44

FURTHER POST-PRISON ADVENTURES

A few days later, I was having lunch with both my moms – my adoptive mom Pat and my birthmother Adele – along with Adele's husband Bill and my wife Linda, at Ricky's ABC Restaurant in Abbotsford. Linda, Pat, and I arrived a few minutes late, having just returned from visiting Pops at the Fleetwood Care Facility in Surrey, where Pops had created his first original "EPG" signed series of drawings using the first half dozen or so of the ninety-six colors of Crayons I had brought him that morning.

Bill and Adele had already secured us a table in the back section of the restaurant, in what I like to call the "kid's section", as it just seems so much less formal than the front area. This felt right, somehow, as I'd been feeling like I was around seven years old again after having spent the past day and a half back in the presence of my adoptive mom.

On our way back from seeing Pops, Mom said to me, "I bet we'll end up paying separately. The last time I had lunch with Bill and Adele they'd insisted on separate bills, as Adele really seems to be watching her pennies."

"Well, Mom," I'd been tempted to joke, "she is Scots-Irish and there's a reason that 'scotch' tends to mean 'miserly.'"

Instead, I simply said, "You do know that Bill's retired, right, as Adele needs him around a lot more now with all of her health issues?"

Mom immediately snapped, "Well, at least neither of them has to pay $3,000 a month for the other's care, like I have to with Pops!"

How quickly I seemed to have forgotten how Mom's entire existence revolved around the narrative of her being the ultimate self-sacrificing martyr, with whom nobody else could ever hope to compete.

It must then have shocked the hell out of Pat when the first words out of Bill's mouth, after "Welcome, everyone," were "Lunch is on me!" This thrilled me on so many levels as I pored over the menu. I proceeded to order a mango shake, the fettucine with some type of German sausages the waitress recommended, along with a side of mac and cheese, and both a strawberry pie and a hot fudge Mount Baker sundae for dessert, hoping I could hide behind this mountain of delights.

Midway through the meal, as I strove to be as silent and invisible as possible, Adele said to Pat, "I can't believe how mobile you are these days! And you recovered so well without any physical therapy?"

It had been just a year and a half since the car crash which had caused Pops to suffer an aortic tear in his heart, and in which Mom's injuries were so severe the doctors weren't sure if she would even walk again.

"It's my strong will and determination which enabled me to do it," proclaimed Pat, "and, of course, God."

"Which played the bigger role, do you think?" Adele gently chided, "Your strong will or God?"

"Well, both," stammered Pat, desperately trying to appear unflustered. "See, when I grew up, we were always told that 'God helps those that help themselves.'"

Wow, I thought to myself. *Could this possibly be the same mom whose voice inside my head on loop saying "your will must be broken, young man" had led me to allow my will to be so broken in my relationship with Joseph that I'd sacrificed my sense of self, and eventually my law license, livelihood, and liberty for him? Yet apparently the biggest lesson she'd learned in the wake of her most recent tragedy was that it was her own will that was most important in saving her.*

It's no wonder that my mom, my adopted sister Shauna, and I had clashed so much throughout our lives. Here you had three stubborn, strong-willed individuals forced to try to co-exist, each determined to demonstrate that their will would prevail. Yet the whole time the person whose will was pre-dominant, our mom, had convinced herself, and my sister and me, that her will was not her own, but that she was instead a self-sacrificing martyr who had spent her entire adult life serving Pops, Shauna, and me, as well as Shauna's three kids, Melissa, Scott and Thomas.

Yet our mom is living proof of why Jesus went to such great lengths to remind us that God desires "mercy, not sacrifice." For sacrifice, like Pat's, creates a sense of entitlement to be loved and sacrificed for in return to such an absurd degree that neither Shauna, nor I, nor Scott, Thomas, nor even Melissa, who calls her grandma twice a day, could ever possibly hope to achieve.

But what this past six and a half years in hell had been slowly forcing me to face was that I'd never measure up to my mom's impossibly high standards of being a self-sacrificing martyr. And I've realized that that was okay. That I needed to learn to be more merciful with myself, just as God has been with me. And that as I slowly learn to be more merciful and forgiving towards myself, hopefully I'll become more merciful, forgiving, and empathetic towards others as well.

Linda and I were in Maui in August/September of 2016 for our anniversary for the first time since the end of my probation earlier that year had granted me the freedom to travel there. After all that we'd been through over the past seven years, Linda thought it best that we bring our passports. Thank God she did. My niece Melissa messaged me near the end of our stay that Pops didn't have much time left. We moved up and rerouted our return flights, with Linda having to return to LA for work, and I, because I had my passport with me, able to fly up to Vancouver.

God, how I loved gazing into Pops' face of love for that timeless time during his last night on earth, as we grasped each other's hands and as we each drew breaths in unison, as together we fulfilled my heart's yearning for

"a shared solitude…

Where 2 souls could swim together in silence

Hearing in each other

The only heartbeat

They'd ever known as home…"

(which came from a poem I'd recently written called "attachment disorder")

And on his last night on earth, Pops continued sharing his beauty until he drew his last breath with "the grateful eight" of us who were gathered around his bedside, consisting of Mom, Shauna, Melissa, Scott, Megan, Thomas, Theresa and me.

And we know that Pops is now celebrating with all of us up in heaven now, and we the grateful eight will all carry with us the radiance of Pops' beautiful soul until we, too, draw our last breaths.

When my mom asked me, on the way to my birthmother Adele's memorial service, seven months after Pops had passed away, "Do you think Adele was saved?" I was shocked. "Of course she was," I replied. "She came back to God through our reunion almost thirty years ago. You know that." When she then responded, "I hope I'm good enough to get into heaven", it broke my heart.

She was still a little girl who could never be good enough for her abusive alcoholic daddy's love, and so could never be good enough for God to love either.

I had spent over forty-five years of my life as a little boy who could never be good enough for either Mom or God to love.

Thank God I went to prison, to enable me to finally begin breaking free from the prison of fear my mom's still trapped in. I hope to God she can manage to break free from it, too.

One Wednesday night, when I decided to hang around for the after-hours portion of the "microphone sessions" poetry/rap/music work-shops, I had no idea just how triggering one of the performances would turn out to be. One of the young artists in the group named Rhythm took the stage and began talking about how his piece was inspired by his having been abused at the age of four by an uncle who happened to be a cop. I'd been sort of lingering in the back, but when I heard his introduction, I felt compelled to move up and join the small group who were gathered in a circle around the stage.

For days after watching him perform that piece I felt incredibly frag-ile, even skirting briefly with the thought of throwing myself off the bridge on my way back from my run a couple of nights later.

It wasn't until I was in my weekly therapy session with Jody that Friday that I finally made the connection. Even though the young guy who performed the piece had been abused when he was four, and my trust was not abused by Joseph until I was in my forties, in many ways it felt even more humiliating to acknowledge having been so abused at such an advanced age, as I'd have thought I'd have learned enough by then how to guard myself against and protect myself from abusers like Joseph.

I had not. Unable to say no to my adoptive mom as a child, after having lost my birthmother and foster mom in first year of my life, I felt like I had to take care of her and protect her from the world, but that no one was ever going to be there to take care of or protect me. When Joseph came along and offered me the chance to be "of counsel" to his thriving immigration consulting firm, I was thrilled, as he seemed to be my knight in shining armor. Here was somebody who clearly needed me, even nicknaming me "The Fireman", just like my mom had needed me.

Unlike my mom, who had been unable to take care of me or protect me because she was too fragile herself, Joseph seemed more than willing to take care of and protect me. He loved taking care of the books for the office, something I hated doing, making sure that all the bills got paid and numbers matched up and that I got paid, too.

From a recent documentary I saw about Nina Simone, however, it seems like I made the same mistake with Joseph that she made with her husband who helped manage her career. What I failed to anticipate was that Joseph would eventually be able to protect me from everyone but himself, and that he was the one person I should have been most afraid of.

I came home and began writing "Triggered," my response to Rhythm's piece. The following Wednesday, I shared it at the next Microphone Sessions. Rhythm's response to my piece was eye-opening. For while I had written about just how fragile and humiliated I had felt having to acknowledge that my trust had been abused when I was in my forties, and that I felt like I should have known better or been able to protect myself better, Rhythm said he'd never thought about abuse at any age being any more or less humiliating than at any other age.

"After all," he said, "we're all babies, aren't we?"

Wow, I thought to myself. *Maybe I should try seeing the world that way for a change.* For we all need love, and we're all vulnerable and fragile and needy. Yet most of my life I'd hidden inside the shell of pretending that I wasn't a baby. No, not me, I'm the strong one. I didn't need nobody for nothin', 'cause nobody was gonna be there for me in the long run anyways. And then when I finally did let down my guard, and told myself, that maybe, just maybe, my friend of twenty years would be there for me, he took that trust and made all the ill-gotten gains he could from it and then threw me under the bus like roadkill.

So now that I'd spent most of the past eight years trying to unlearn as many of the lies that had sustained me for most of the previous forty-six years as I possibly could, perhaps that's as good a place to start as any other.

We're all babies.

We all need love.

We're all needy, fragile and vulnerable.

Nobody knows nothin'.

Most of us spend far too much of our lives hiding behind masks, trying to pretend that we know what the hell we're doing, and what the hell is going on, hoping against hope that the masks don't slip, lest anyone catch a glimpse of just how child-like our souls really are.

So let the masks slip.

Let our souls swim free.

Let the world see just how child-like we are.

Don't be surprised, though, if two-thirds of our fellow humans draw back in horror and make sure their masks are more firmly secured than ever. That's their prison, not ours.

For as we begin to tear down the walls of fear that have been suffocating our souls for far too long now, we will hopefully find ourselves being able to dance delightedly once again in the playground of love which is, after all, our soul's true home.

For the past five years or so, ever since I took that Writing the Healing Story class with Barbara Abercrombie in the fall of 2012, I'd been trying my best to tackle this monstrous marathon of a memoir. Now once again, I found myself needing to look back for the motivation and inspiration to move forward. For way back in the spring of 1988, almost thirty years ago now, I managed to win a blue ribbon by finishing in the top third of the LA Marathon, despite running with both my knees wrapped and my formerly broken right ankle wrapped to mask the pain.

As I struggled to break through the pain barrier this time to finish this draft of my memoir, I hoped to God this could be my best year ever in WriterWorld.

None of us should be defined by the worst thing we've ever done, or I would run the risk of going to my grave cursing myself for having so fully surrendered my power as a lawyer to Joseph that I would end up being stripped of that power. For during those years I worked with Joseph, I was no longer faithful in my exercise of my power as a lawyer, and as a result I had now been humbled and forced to acknowledge that I was no better than the most depraved of criminals, but rather just fortunate to have been allowed this opportunity for awakening.

I almost didn't go to church this morning. I tried resetting the alarm for another hour, but God kept rattling around inside my head, refusing to let me stay in bed. I finally, grudgingly, took the hint, showered, shaved, brushed my teeth, threw on my Gulag t-shirt (with the Solzhenitsyn quote about "the dividing line between good and evil being in each one of our hearts") and Dockers and headed out the door.

I drove for a about ten minutes to the Westside Vineyard Church, first listening to some hip-hop, and then switching over to an electronic dance music station. I loved the last song that was playing as I parked a few blocks from the church, especially the line which went, "I love the beauty of your insanity."

The sermon, which was part of a series called "Conversations with Jesus", was entitled "The real place we meet God." Our pastor, Brad Bailey, took as his text the story found in Matthew 15: 21-28 of the Gentile woman from Tyre and Sidon who came to see Jesus when he visited her region and asked for her daughter to be freed from a demon that had possessed her, and Jesus did so in response to her great faith.

At the point in the sermon where I came in, Brad was talking about how this woman's truly great faith was demonstrated by her belief, not in her merits, but in God's mercy. This reminded me of a time when my faith had been severely tested, and I came to the painful realization that I'd spent most of my life believing the lie that my initials, "KEDG", stood for "Kelly Entirely Dependent upon Goodness", instead of what they truly stood for, which was "Kelly Entirely Dependent upon Grace."

Brad then went on to pose three questions. The first was: "Do we embrace our need for mercy and grace?" He followed that question up with examples of those who clearly did, like the publican who went into the temple and simply prayed, "Lord, be merciful to me, a sinner", and the prodigal son who, upon returning to his father, said, "I am no longer worthy to be called your son; make me like one of your hired servants."

Brad then reminded us of the passage found in Isaiah 53:6: "We all, like sheep, have gone astray, each of us has turned to our own way." I was reminded of the countless times throughout my life that God had cared for me despite what a stupid sheep I'd been, as I had gone astray far more times than I could ever begin to count. I, like all my fellow humans, am fundamentally self-oriented. Tim Keller expressed the paradox of the human condition beautifully when he wrote "We're far worse than we ever imagined, and far more loved than we could ever dream."

Brad's second question was, "Do we express our need for mercy and grace?" This is something I had been striving to do in my writing, and when sharing my vulnerability with those precious few souls I felt safe enough to be that open with.

Brad's third and final question was, "Do we extend the need for mercy and grace to others?" For as Matthew 5:7 reminds us, "Blessed are the merciful, for they will be shown mercy."

Brad then closed with a couple of Martin Luther's most powerful quotes. The first was, "Now, I should like to know whether your soul, tired of its own righteousness, is learning to be revived by and to trust in the righteousness of Christ... Beware of aspiring to such purity that you will not wish to be looked upon as a sinner, or to be one. For Christ dwells only in sinners."

The second was found on a handwritten note in his pocket when he died: "This is true. We are all beggars."

I was weeping as we sang the closing song by Matt Redman, entitled "Mercy," especially the lines "Mercy, mercy, as endless as the sea." I then headed off to take my Farmers' Market berries to the car before returning for after-service prayer. I had noticed my documentary filmmaker friend Jason and his wife Julia sitting up on the left side of the church before I left, and silently begged God that Julia might still be around by the time I got back to pray with me, as I knew what an amazing prayer warrior she was. When I returned and headed to the front to get my communion crackers and grape juice, I was thrilled to see that not only was Julia still around, but she was part of the after-service prayer team, which I'd never even realized she'd been a part of before.

I waited impatiently for her to finish praying with the guy she'd been praying with when I returned. Fortunately for me, her two oldest sons, Rain and Micah, aged eight and six, were even more impatient than I, and kept coming up to see how their mom was doing. Julia eventually managed to wrap up that prayer session, and she was then free to pray for me.

I shared with her how I'd been more afraid than I'd been in ages lately, as I was more broke than I'd ever been in my life, having not had any new Canadian immigration clients in months. We kneeled and prayed for quite some time. Julia's prayer reflected that God had clearly shown her that one of my greatest struggles had been trying to earn the right to not be abandoned by trying to play God by sacrificing myself for others.

I then shared with her about how I'd been shockingly reminded of how much I'd absorbed my adoptive mom's fear-based, angry God legalism last spring, when she told me she hoped that she was "good enough" to make it into heaven. Julia immediately sensed my need for a prayer of blessing.

Julia then proceeded to pray for me a second time.

She opened by saying, "I'm sorry I couldn't be the mother you needed me to be. Please forgive me for all the times I made you feel unworthy."

"I didn't realize you needed to be forgiven for anything, but yeah, sure, I forgive you." I was confused. Julia was a great mom to her three kids. What could she possibly be asking my forgiveness for? As she continued to pray, however, I gradually came to realize that this time around, she was playing the role of my mom, and asking for my forgiveness for all the times she'd made me feel like I was unworthy of God's love. This prayer of blessing was incredibly powerful and healing for me.

As she neared the end of it, she asked me if God had given me any visions. I told her that I had seen both Pops, my adoptive dad, and Adele, my birthmother, who died a year and half ago and ten months ago, respectively, laughing and celebrating in heaven as I basked in the blessing of being God's beloved son, through this prayer of my beloved friend Julia. Julia then asked if I felt the need for a father's embrace, and when I nodded yes, she asked our friend Bobby, who was sitting just to the side of us, to give me a hug, and we embraced warmly.

Mom and I never talked for more than about five minutes during our weekly Sunday calls. Whenever I'd start to go deep, Mom would talk about the weather. On Palm Sunday, 2020, that dynamic suddenly shifted.

"How've you felt, Mom, being so isolated with the Coronavirus lockdown?" I asked.

"Your sister's been so caring. She teamed up with Melissa, Scott, and Thomas and bought me a tablet. Then she helped me figure out to use it so I could have FaceTime with the family."

I'd been afraid when I'd first heard that my sister had even set up a Facebook page for her, as I didn't want mom to see my Facebook posts, for fear I might edit myself for her.

"Shauna also bought Crayons for me, just like we did for Pops," Mom continued.

"My therapist Jody had me go buy some Crayons and a sketch pad too, Mom."

Mom and I then managed to talk for over half an hour without her once mentioning the weather. Having just written and posted "Love in the time of Coronavirus", where I acknowledged that I was a terrified six-year-old, but that I felt that I was now living on a planet full of terrified six-year-olds, had finally freed me to have my first real adult conversation with my mom in my entire life.

She even talked briefly about the hell her childhood had been as the only child of an abusive alcoholic Irish father.

"Was Grandpa Bob ever violent?" I asked.

"Not towards me," she answered quietly.

"Did he ever hit your mom?"

"Mom really knew how to push his buttons, son".

Rather than challenge her for once again "blaming the victim", I let the moment pass.

Now that my mom and I have finally begun to see ourselves as terrified six-year-olds who'd always felt we could never be good enough for a godlike parent's love, my hope was that we might continue our healing journey together. I'd wanted this more than anything since I started writing this memoir. I thanked God for the healing work that had enabled us to at least begin the process of truly beginning to see ourselves, and each other, and by doing so, to begin the process of forgiving ourselves, and each other. Forgiveness truly is the hardest part of the spiritual journey, but at least I felt like we'd now made a start down that road.

CHAPTER 45

LETTER TO MY MOM
AKA: FROM GOODNESS TO GRACE

When you told me, Mom, on our way to my birth mom Adele's memorial service, that you hoped you were "good enough" to get into heaven, it broke my heart. None of us is good enough. But God doesn't care if we're good enough.

God wants you to know that you're loved. God wants you to know that you bring joy. But most of all, God wants you to love yourself.

God wants you to forgive yourself for not being able to protect your mom, my Grandma Millie, when your dad, my Grandpa Bob, would come home drunk from the bar. You were only a kid, after all.

You couldn't save your dad from the bottle.

You couldn't save your mom from your dad's abuse.

But you did love them dearly. Just like you loved Pops dearly. Just like you've loved Shauna and me dearly, your grandkids dearly, and your great-grandkids dearly.

You just need to learn to start focusing more of your energy on loving and forgiving yourself.

So quit asking yourself the wrong question.

No, you're not good enough to get into heaven, and never will be.

None of us is, and none of us ever will be.

Do you love God?

Do you love your neighbor?

But most importantly, do you love, and can you forgive, yourself?

If the answer to all three is yes, then you're already in heaven.

I had lost Pops in the fall of 2016, and lost my birthmother in the spring of 2017. I would sometimes tease Linda that she's not allowed to die, as I need her to still be around when I finish my third memoir, as I'll be dedicating it to her. I had no desire to ever hear from or about Joseph again. The old me that had so desperately needed him that I lost myself in the process, had died. A new me was in the process of being born.

CHAPTER 46

HELLO TO MY NEW LIFE

One day during the first few months of the coronavirus pandemic, as I made my way over to the condo mailroom to see if my Amnesty International bandana masks needed to be replenished, a neighbor and I both noticed a couple of police cruisers parked out front. As I opened the front gate to let my neighbor and his daughter in, he joked, "I wonder if they're here for me," and mimed being handcuffed. I laughed and said, "Better you than me, my friend!"

As I waited outside the mailroom for another neighbor to exit, honoring the social distancing etiquette which had been in effect since the coronavirus lockdown had begun forty-five days earlier, with my own Amnesty International bandana loosely draped around my neck, and rocking my new black and white "Make Love Great Again" hat and my new red and black "War is Peace/Freedom is Slavery/Ignorance is Strength" t-shirt, I noticed four cops, unmasked as I was, strolling down the hall towards me.

"Everything okay?" I asked casually.

"All good," one of them answered as they passed by.

And just like that, a story that had begun with a bang ten years, six months, and nineteen days earlier, with four heavily armed ICE agents, banging on our condo door early on the morning of October 15, 2009, and had continued with my being cuffed and arrested by a dozen heavily armed ICE agents at LAX later that same day, now ended with a whimper. This was the sort of encounter with law enforcement that would drive no one to write a book about it. Instead, it was a simple interaction involving five unmasked humans during the coronavirus pandemic of 2020, four of whom just happened to be law enforcement. I suddenly realized that the cops I'd been most afraid of my whole life had been the cops inside my own head. If my old life had disowned me in the fall of 2009, my new life beckoned to me now.

ACKNOWLEDGMENTS

I would like to thank my editor, the *New York Times* bestselling author and wonderful storyteller Caroline Leavitt. I would also like to thank Eric Myers, the first agent I pitched to at the Santa Barbara Writers Conference who truly got what I was trying to do with this book. In addition, I would like to thank my logo designer McKenna DeBont, my artist photographers Jason Uriel Parker and Julia Parker, as well as Gordon McLellan and his team at Dartfrog Books/Canoe Tree Press for helping me get this book out into the world.

Thanks as well to my beta readers, D.M. Peterson, Jennifer Dodge, Judit Maull, and Skinner Myers. I would also like to thank my ARC readers & reviewers, including Andy Behrman, Judit Maull, Deanna Pak, Matt Pallamary, Bill Watanabe, Judge Mary Beth O'Connor, Trey Dowell, D.M. Peterson, Skinner Myers, Mimi Zhao, Andrew Sandoval, Jacqueline Snow, Elizabeth Gordon and August Norman.

Thanks so much to USC Law Professor Jody Armour, who invited me to give a talk to his law students, which I entitled "Heart Surgery for the Legal Profession", which was very well received, and helped inspire me to continue this decade long odyssey. Jody also introduced me to Aim4theHeart, which features a poetry/hiphop workshop called Mic Sessions hosted in his home which is led by Leila Steinberg, who used to be Tupac Shakur's manager, as well as Heart Sessions, which is hosted by Marisol Ibanez-Tintorer down in Long Beach, a weekly workshop which I continue to be a part of to this day, and which continues to inspire and amaze me.

I am beyond grateful for the instructors and classmates in the countless memoir and other writing classes I've taken at UCLA Extension over the years, including Erika Schickel, Shawna Kenney, Monica Holloway, and Elizabeth Silver. I would also like to thank the many wonderful workshop leaders and fellow writers I've gotten to know over the past decade at the Santa Barbara Writers Conference, including Matt Pallamary, Monte Schultz and Lorelei Armstrong, as well as the priceless feedback from the University Club Writers Group made up of writers I met at the SBWC and who I was blessed to be a part of a monthly writers group with for almost seven years, including Angela Borda, Calla and Jeremy Gold, Lisa Lamb, Nate Streeper, Rachael Quisel, Sharon Whatley, Sia Morhardt, Kara Mae Brown, Melissa Clare Wright, Christine Logsdon and Yvette Keller.

My gratitude knows no bounds for all those amazing crowdfunding donors who showed such faith in me and enabled me to both raise the necessary funds to hire my editor, as well as much of the funding I needed to be able to hire Dartfrog Books/CanoeTree Press to assist me in getting this book published. For the Editor Campaign, those included Platinum Donors Noura Alfadl-Andreasson and William Priestley, Gold Donors Rey Finnegan, Eric Inouye, Ken Downing and Shell Small, Silver Donors Jane Oak and Matthew Spaulding, Bronze Donors Dixie Mitchell, Mabel Harman, Maggie Stewart, Martin Trupiano, Bill Watanabe, and Elly Levy, and Editor Donors Johanna Yukiko Haneda, Lana Dvorak, and Daria Iakovleva. For the Hybrid Publisher/Assisted Self-Publishing Campaign, those included Silver Donor Noura Alfadl-Andreasson, Bronze Donors Mina Tran, Olivia Liu, and Bill Watanabe, Hybrid Donor + Donors Deanna Pak, Eugene Pidgeon, Jane Oak and Laz Machado, and Hybrid Donors Linnette Ling, Veronika Syrop, and Amanda Hopper, as well as well as numerous other donors who gave so sacrificially to these campaigns.

As mentioned in the dedications, I would not be here today without my adoptive mom Pat having loved me the best she could, and without my adoptive dad Eldon (aka: Pops), having loved me better than I could love myself. I would also not be here today without at least two other people who also loved me better than I could love myself, my birth-mother Adele, whose love for me will be at the heart of my upcoming memoir *Finding Heart*, and my soulmate Linda, who hung in there with me throughout all of the darkness detailed in these pages, and whose love for me will be the centerpiece of the concluding memoir of my trilogy, *Finding Soul*.

ABOUT THE AUTHOR

Kelly Giles obtained his Juris Doctor Degree from Pepperdine University School of Law in 1989. Kelly practiced U.S. immigration law for twenty-three years, until late 2012, and continues to practice Canadian immigration law. He self-published his Darwin's Desert trilogy of poetry books between 2010 and 2012, *Swimming in a Thunderstorm*, *Surfing the Tsunami* and *Surrendering to Transcendence*, and has published multiple Six Word Memoirs on the *Smith Magazine* website. In 2014, he gave a talk entitled "Heart Surgery for the Legal Profession" to a class of USC Law Professor Jody Armour's law school students related to his upcoming memoir. He also performed as a featured poet at both Cobalt Poets and at Michael Jasorka's *Hello World* Zine Release Party, and has been a featured guest on both Jill Delbridge's *Artist's Lounge* podcast and Apryl Skies's *Edgar Allen Poet* podcast. For the past several years, he has been a member of Aim for the Heart's Microphone Sessions and Heart Sessions poetry and hip-hop workshops, founded by Tupac Shakur's manager Leila Steinberg in 1996. He currently lives in Culver City, California, volunteers with Amnesty International, Reverb and Headcount, and is a member of UCLA Extension's Writer's Program Now, Film Independent, and NewFilmMakers LA. *Killing Justice* is his debut memoir. He is passionate about raising awareness about mental illness and the criminal justice system and encouraging others on their healing journey, especially through the arts. You can read more of his work at www.kellygiles.com.

A NOTE FROM THE AUTHOR

Thanks so much for reading my debut memoir *Killing Justice*. Please feel free to share my website www.kellygiles.com with all your friends and social media networks, and be sure and sign up for my email list for monthly updates, and connect with me and drop me a line on social media:

- Instagram: https://www.instagram.com/kellyab303/
- Facebook Personal Page: https://www.facebook.com/profile.php?id=100077323377913
- Facebook Writer's Page: https://m.facebook.com/people/Kelly -Giles-Artist-Page/100086023074255/
- LinkedIn: https://www.linkedin.com/in/kelly-giles-0260269/
- Twitter/X: https://twitter.com/kellyab33

Also, please feel free to check out my three volumes of poetry at https://www.lulu.com/spotlight/kellyab3/.

If you enjoyed the book, please consider taking a moment to write me a positive review on the sales platform or review site of your choice, as it helps indie authors like myself.

Finally, please be sure and stay tuned for my upcoming memoir *Finding Heart*.

www.ingramcontent.com/pod-product-compliance
Lightning Source LLC
Chambersburg PA
CBHW021716120626
46545CB00004B/1581